Lecture Notes in Computer S

Commenced Publication in 1973
Founding and Former Series Editors:
Gerhard Goos, Juris Hartmanis, and Jan van Leeuwen

Editorial Board

Maria Papadopouli   Philippe Owezarski
Aiko Pras (Eds.)

Traffic Monitoring and Analysis

First International Workshop, TMA 2009
Aachen, Germany, May 11, 2009
Proceedings

 Springer

Volume Editors

Maria Papadopouli
University of Crete, Dept. of Computer Science
P.O. Box 2208, 714 09, Heraklion, Crete, Greece
and
F.O.R.T.H., Institute of Computer Science
Vassilika Vouton, P.O. Box 1385, 711 10, Heraklion, Greece
E-mail: mgp@ics.forth.gr

Philippe Owezarski
LAAS – CNRS
7 Avenue du Colonel Roche, 31077 Toulouse, cedex 4, France
E-mail: owe@laas.fr

Aiko Pras
University of Twente
Dept. of Electrical Engineering, Mathematics and Computer Science
Design and Analysis of Communication Systems Group
P.O. Box 217, 7500 AE Enschede, The Netherlands
E-mail: a.pras@utwente.nl

Library of Congress Control Number: Applied for

CR Subject Classification (1998): C.2, D.4.4, H.3, H.4

LNCS Sublibrary: SL 5 – Computer Communication Networks and
Telecommunications

ISSN   0302-9743

ISBN   978-3-642-01644-8 Springer Berlin Heidelberg New York

springer.com

© Springer-Verlag Berlin Heidelberg 2009

Typesetting: Camera-ready by author, data conversion by Scientific Publishing Services, Chennai, India
Printed on acid-free paper   SPIN: 12672158   06/3180   5 4 3 2 1 0

Foreword

The First International Workshop on Traffic Monitoring and Analysis (TMA 2009) was an initiative from the COST Action IC0703 "Data Traffic Monitoring and Analysis: Theory, Techniques, Tools and Applications for the Future Networks" (www.cost-tma.eu).

The COST program is an intergovernmental framework for European Cooperation in Science and Technology, allowing the coordination of nationally funded research on a European level. Each COST Action contributes to reducing the fragmentation in research and opening the European Research Area to cooperation worldwide.

Traffic monitoring and analysis (TMA) is now an important research topic within the field of networking. It involves many research groups worldwide that are collectively advancing our understanding of the Internet.

The importance of TMA research is motivated by the fact that modern packet networks are highly complex and ever-evolving objects. Understanding, developing and managing such environments is difficult and expensive in practice. Traffic monitoring is a key methodology for understanding telecommunication technology and improving its operation, and the recent advances in this field suggest that evolved TMA-based techniques can play a key role in the operation of real networks. Moreover, TMA offers a basis for prevention and response in network security, as typically the detection of attacks and intrusions requires the analysis of detailed traffic records.

On the more theoretical side, TMA is an attractive research topic for many reasons. First, the inherent complexity of the Internet has attracted many researchers to face traffic measurements since the pioneering times. Second, TMA offers a fertile ground for theoretical and cross-disciplinary research—think of the various analysis techniques being imported into TMA from other fields—while at the same time providing a clear perspective for the exploitation of the results in real network environments. In other words, TMA research has the potential to reconcile theoretical investigations with practical applications, and to realign curiosity-driven with problem-driven research.

In the spirit of the COST program, the COST-TMA Action was launched in 2008 to promote building a research community in the specific field of TMA. Today, it involves 50+ research groups from academic and industrial organizations in 23 countries. In its first year the Action promoted a number of research exchanges mostly involving young researchers. A portal dedicated to TMA research is being set in place which aims at becoming a reference point for the research community in the field, in Europe and beyond (www.tma-portal.eu).

The TMA 2009 workshop marked an important moment in the lifetime of the (still young!) COST-TMA Action. The success of this first workshop—witnessed by the number of submissions and quality of the presented works—is very promising about the future development of the TMA workshop series into one of the reference venues for the larger research community in this field.

March 2009   Fabio Ricciato

Preface

The First International Workshop on Traffic Monitoring and Analysis (TMA 2009) was an initiative from the COST Action IC0703 "Data Traffic Monitoring and Analysis (TMA): Theory, Techniques, Tools and Applications for the Future Networks" granted by the European Commission.

This TMA workshop extends the COST-TMA research and discussions to the world-wide community of researchers in the area of traffic monitoring and analysis. For this purpose, the TMA 2009 technical Program Committee selected the best papers submitted to the TMA 2009 workshop. Specifically, 15 out of the 34 submitted papers were accepted for publication in the workshop proceedings and were presented during a full-day event. They encompass research areas related to traffic analysis and classification, measurements, topology discovery, detection of specific applications and events, packet inspection, and traffic inference. In order to grant a long life and a high-visibility level to the TMA workshop, the proceedings of the TMA 2009 workshop are published by Springer in the LNCS series.

We address our sincere thanks to the technical Program Committee members for their diligence and hard work during the reviewing process, as well as to Springer for accepting to be the TMA workshop series publisher.

We are also very thankful to Michel Mandjes from CWI in The Netherlands, who accepted to give the keynote talk of this workshop on "Traffic Models, and Their Use in Provisioning and Traffic Management."

This year, the workshop was organized as a full-day event on the first day of the IFIP Networking conference. We would like to thank its organizers and patrons for accepting the TMA workshop as a joint event. In particular, we are grateful to Otto Spaniol for his generous support while preparing the workshop.

We hope you enjoy the proceedings.

March 2009

Maria Papadopouli
Philippe Owezarski
Aiko Pras
Udo Krieger

Organization

Technical Program Committee

Pierre Borgnat	ENS Lyon
Prosper Chemouil	France Telecom R&D
Jean-Laurent Costeux	France Telecom R&D
Xenofontas Dimitropoulos	ETH Zurich
Constantine Dovrolis	Georgia Tech
Michalis Faloutsos	University of California at Riverside
Timur Friedman	UPMC Paris University and CNRS
Nuno M. Garcia	CICANT, ULHT, Lisbon, Portugal
James Hong	Postech Korea
Gianluca Iannaccone	Intel Research Berkeley
Lucjan Janowski	AGH University of Science and Technology
Merkourios Karaliopoulos	ETH Zurich
Jasleen Kaur	University of North Carolina at Chapel Hill
Evangelos Markatos	University of Crete and FORTH
Sandor Molnar	Budapest University of Technology and Economics
Jordi Domingo-Pascual	Universitat Politècnica de Catalunya
Kostas Pentikousis	VTT Technical Research Centre of Finland
Fabio Ricciato	University of Salento
Dario Rossi	ENST Telecom Paris
Luca Salgarelli	University of Brescia
Kave Salamatian	Lancaster University
Don Smith	University of North Carolina at Chapel Hill
Tanja Tzeby	Fraunhofer FOKUS
Steve Uhlig	T-labs/TU Berlin
Artur Ziviani	LNCC Brazil

Local Organizer

Udo Krieger	Otto Friedrich University Bamberg

Technical Program Committee Co-chairs

Philippe Owezarski	LAAS-CNRS, National Centre for Scientific Research
Maria Papadopouli	University of Crete and FORTH
Aiko Pras	University of Twente

Table of Contents

QoS Measurement

Rupture Detection

Traffic Classification

Traffic Analysis and Topology Measurements

Realistic Passive Packet Loss Measurement for High-Speed Networks

Aleš Friedl[1], Sven Ubik[1], Alexandros Kapravelos[2], Michalis Polychronakis[2], and Evangelos P. Markatos[2]

[1] CESNET, Czech Republic
{afriedl,ubik}@cesnet.cz
[2] FORTH-ICS, Greece
{kapravel,mikepo,markatos}@ics.forth.gr

Abstract. Realistic and accurate packet loss measurement of production traffic has been challenging, since the frequently-used active monitoring approaches using probe packets cannot capture the packet loss experienced by the traffic of *individual* user applications. In this paper, we present a new approach for the accurate measurement of the packet loss rate faced by actual production traffic based on passive network monitoring. In contrast to previous work, our method is able to pinpoint the packet loss rate experienced by the *individual* traffic flows of concurrently running applications. Experimental results suggest that our approach measures packet loss with 100% accuracy for network speeds as high as 12 Gbit/s, while traditional ICMP-based approaches were usually much less accurate. We also report experiences from a real-world deployment of our method in several 10 Gbit/s links of European research networks, where it has been successfully operational for several months.

1 Introduction

Packet loss is an important performance characteristic of network traffic, crucial for applications including long-range data transfers, video and audio transmission, as well as distributed and GRID computing. Unfortunately, most of the existing tools report only *network link* packet loss rate and cannot measure the actual packet loss experienced by the traffic of *individual* applications. Most of the existing techniques are based on active network monitoring, which involves the injection of probe packets into the network for measuring how many of them eventually reach their final destination [2, 10, 11]. Although these approaches approximate the overall packet loss of a link, they inherently cannot measure the packet loss faced by the traffic of individual applications. To make matters worse, for accurately approximating bursty and volatile packet loss events, active monitoring methods need to inject a large number of packets, increasing their intrusiveness in the network, and possibly perturbing the dynamics of the system. When using a small number of probe packets to avoid a high level of intrusiveness, such methods need to run for a long period, and then are only able to approximate packet loss rates that remain constant for a long duration—a highly unlikely case in real networks.

In contrast to active monitoring approaches, in this paper we describe a real-time end-to-end packet loss measurement method for high-speed networks based on distributed

M. Papadopouli, P. Owezarski, and A. Pras (Eds.): TMA 2009, LNCS 5537, pp. 1–7, 2009.

passive network monitoring. The main benefit of the proposed approach is the accurate measurement of the *actual* packet loss faced by user traffic, both in terms of loss magnitude, as well as the identification of the individual traffic flows that were affected. Such fine-grained per-application packet loss measurement is important in case different applications on the same network path exhibit different degrees of packet loss, e.g., due to the deployment of differentiated services and service level agreements (SLAs), rate-limiting devices, or load-balancing configurations.

We presented a prototype version of a passive packet loss estimation method in our previous work [9]. In this paper, we describe a significantly enhanced version, called PcktLoss, that measures packet loss with higher precision, can detect even very short packet loss events, and has been proved to work reliably for multi-Gigabit traffic in a real-world deployment at the GÉANT2 network, which interconnects most of the national research and education networks (NRENs) in Europe.

2   Related Work

Ping is one of the most popular tools for inferring basic network characteristics, such as round-trip time and packet loss. Ping sends ICMP probe packets to a target host at fixed intervals, and reports loss when the response packets are not received within a specified time period. Although ping has been used as a first-cut mechanism for link packet loss estimation, its applicability has recently started to get limited because several routers and firewalls drop or rate-limit ICMP packets, which introduces *artificial* packet loss that undermines the accuracy of the measurement. Instead of using ICMP packets, zing [2] and Badabing [11] estimate end-to-end packet loss in one direction between two cooperative end hosts by sending UDP packets at pre-specified time intervals. Sting [10] overcomes the limitation of requiring two cooperative hosts by measuring the link loss rate from a client to any TCP-based server on the Internet based on the loss recovery algorithms of the TCP protocol.

Benko and Veres have proposed a TCP packet loss measurement approach based on monitoring sequence numbers in TCP packets [4]. Our approach uses a completely different estimation approach, independent from the L4 protocol specification, and thus can be universally applied to both TCP and UDP connections. Ohta and Miyazaki [8] have explored a passive monitoring technique for packet loss estimation relying on hash-based packet identification. Their work is similar to our approach, but ours differs in that it matches packets to flows and compares flows with each other for computing the packet loss, while theirs hashes the packet's payload and correlates them. Our approach is more lightweight and thus can be performed on-line, while Ohta and Miyazaki's technique needs to stop monitoring for computing the packet loss.

3   Architecture

Over the past few years, we have been witnessing an increasing deployment of passive network monitoring sensors all over Europe. In this paper, we propose to capitalize on the proliferation of passive monitoring sensors and use them to perform accurate per-application packet loss measurements. Our approach is quite simple: assuming a

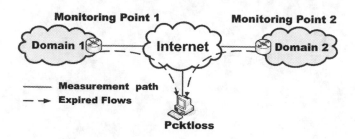

Fig. 1. Overall architecture of PcktLoss

network path equipped with two passive monitoring sensors at its endpoints, as shown in Fig. 1, measuring packet loss is just a matter of subtraction: by subtracting the number of packets arrived at the destination from the number of packets that were originally sent, one can find exactly how many packets were lost in the network.

Unfortunately, our algorithm is a little more complicated than what we have simplistically described. Indeed, the timing details of the subtraction are crucial for the correct calculation of the loss rate. A prematurely computed subtraction may report as lost all packets that have left their source but have not yet reached their destination. To accurately define the timing of the subtraction, we base our method on the concept of *expired flows*. A flow is defined as the set of IP packets with the same L4 protocol, source and destination IP address, and source and destination port (also known as a 5-tuple). A flow is considered *expired* if no packet has arrived within a specified timeout (30 sec in our experiments). This differs from the traditional Netflow or IPFIX flow records, which also report long-running flows. In case of TCP, a flow can also be considered expired when the connection is explicitly closed, i.e., when an RST of FIN packet is seen.

To calculate per-application packet loss, our algorithm periodically retrieves the expired flows from the two passive monitoring sensors at the endpoints of the network path. Each record includes a flow identifier (the 5-tuple), the number of packets and transferred bytes, as well as the TTL and timestamp of the first packet of the flow. If the same expired flow is reported from both sensors, but with a different number of packets, then this is an indication that the flow lost some packets, and the actual packet loss rate can be computed from the difference of the reported number of packets. Flows with only one packet captured are ignored, since they will not be matched if their packet is lost. This limitation derives from the fact that we are not always sure if this traffic is routed through our observation points. Therefor we cannot deside if the packet was lost or avoided all other observation points.

4   Experimental Evaluation

4.1   Comparison with Active Monitoring

Our experiments aim to explore the accuracy of PcktLoss compared to ping, probably the most widely used packet loss measurement tool based on active monitoring, as well as verify that our method measures the actual packet loss of existing traffic without

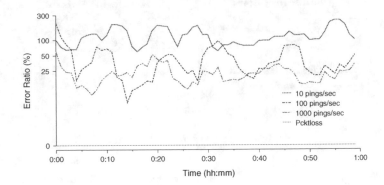

Fig. 2. Measurement error for `ping` and `PcktLoss` when introducing a constant loss rate of 0.1%. `PcktLoss` reports the actual loss rate without deviations.

deviations. Our experimental environment consists of two PCs, a "sender" and a "receiver," also acting as passive monitoring sensors for `PcktLoss`. The traffic between the two sensors is transparently forwarded through a third PC that introduces artificial packet loss at a controlled rate using `netem` [6]. We generated UDP traffic with `mgen` [3], which uses explicit sequence numbers and logging at both ends to calculate the actual number of lost packets. We used 1 Mbit/s traffic with 1KB packets to prevent the passive monitors from dropping packets due to excessive load, since both sensors used commodity Ethernet interfaces. Each run lasted for one hour.

In our experiment, we introduce a constant packet loss rate of 0.1% to all traffic between the two sensors. Figure 2 presents the measurement error ratio for `ping` using different probe sending rates, as well as for `PcktLoss`. The error ratio is calculated based on the packet loss reported by `mgen`. As expected, the lower `ping`'s probe sending rate, the higher its measurement error. Even when using an aggressive rate of 1000 probe packets per second, `ping` still cannot accurately measure the actual packet loss. In contrast, `PcktLoss` measures the actual packet loss without errors.

It is possible for a network path to exhibit packet loss only for certain classes of traffic, e.g., due to a traffic shaping policy. In this case, the probe traffic of an active monitoring tool may not face the same packet loss as the production traffic.

4.2   Runtime Performance

We tested the performance of `PcktLoss` under heavy traffic load in the controlled environment shown in Fig. 3. We used the Ixia 1600 packet generator and analyser to send and receive traffic at a 10 Gbit/s rate. The traffic passes through a custom FPGA-based device that introduces artificial packet loss by selectively dropping packets at a specified rate. The traffic before entering and after leaving the packet loss emulator is diverted through optical splitters to two DAG8.2 monitoring cards installed on a PC running Linux and MAPI, while `PcktLoss` runs on a different PC. Both PCs are equipped with two quad-core 3 GHz Intel Xeon Woodcrest CPUs.

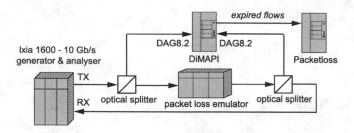

Fig. 3. Experimental environment for performance testing

Table 1. PcktLoss throughput

Generated rate for both links	Processed packets
10 Gbit/s	100 %
12 Gbit/s	100 %
14 Gbit/s	99.44 %
16 Gbit/s	90.11 %
18 Gbit/s	79.65 %
20 Gbit/s	72.19 %

Table 2. PcktLoss precision

Emulated loss rate	# packets dropped by the emulator	# lost packets as reported by PcktLoss
10^{-2}	14000000	14000000
10^{-3}	1400000	1400000
10^{-4}	140000	140000
10^{-5}	14000	14000
10^{-6}	1400	1400
10^{-7}	146	146

We configured the packet generator to send 500 UDP and 500 TCP flows using varying packet sizes according to the RFC2544 [5]. The throughput achieved for different traffic rates is presented in Table 1. For speeds up to 12 Gbit/s, PcktLoss processed 100% of the traffic without dropping any packets. Note that the monitoring sensor had to process twice the traffic from both monitoring cards. If each card were installed on a separate PC, it should be possible to monitor full 10 Gb/s of traffic.

In our next set of experiments, we ran a series of tests by setting the packet loss emulator to introduce a loss rate ranging from 10^{-2} to 10^{-7}. On each run, the traffic generator transmitted $1.4 * 10^9$ packets at a speed of 5 Gbit/s. As shown in Table 2, in all cases PcktLoss was able to measure the exact number of lost packets. For a loss rate of 10^{-7} the emulator actually dropped slightly more packets. We doubly verified the precision of the results reported by PcktLoss by comparing them with the actual number of lost packets as reported both by the packet loss generator, as well as by the traffic generator which also receives back the generated traffic.

5   Real-world Deployment

We have installed PcktLoss on several sensors deployed in the GN2 network, which interconnects the National Research and Educational Networks (NRENs) of most European countries. The networks involved in monitoring are CESNET, PIONIER, SWITCH, connected by 10 Gbit/s links, and ACAD, which is connected by a 1 Gbit/s link.

The runtime performance of PcktLoss in this deployment is summarized in Table 3, which presents statistics for one week of continuous monitoring. Traffic load

Table 3. Passive and active loss measurements and PcktLoss performance

Monitoring station	max 5-min traffic load [Mb/s]	5-min CPU load [%]	packets processed in 1 week	packets dropped in 1 week
SWITCH out	2800	10+10 (2 cores)	$1.62 * 10^{10}$	0
SWITCH in	6800	40+20 (2 cores)	$8.33 * 10^{10}$	0
PIONIER out	240	5	$1.55 * 10^9$	83991
PIONIER in	370	20	$2.00 * 10^9$	5083
ACAD in+out	535	40	$3.30 * 10^9$	0
CESNET in+out	440	90	$1.64 * 10^{10}$	344796
Total			$1.23 * 10^{11}$	433870

refers to the maximum load among all 5-minute intervals over the week. The indicated CPU load was measured during the same interval. The monitoring cards on the two most loaded links did not drop any packets and the CPUs were not fully utilized, which demonstrates the scalability of our approach. There were occasional packet drops on three of the sensors due to known configuration shortcomings: the CESNET sensor has much slower memory, while the DAG cards in PIONIER use the PCI-X bus, which cannot transfer traffic bursts without dropping packets. It should be noted that PcktLoss was just one of three concurrently running passive monitoring applications on the same sensor. Each sensor also hosted ABW [12] to monitor short-term traffic load and distribution into protocols, and Burst [13] to quantify traffic burstiness. Particularly ABW is quite CPU-intensive, since it performs header-based classification for all packets and payload searching for selected packets.

Overall, PcktLoss reported 2,737,177 lost packets (out of which 433,870 were dropped by the monitoring cards due to overload), corresponding to an actual packet loss rate of $2.22 * 10^{-5}$. Most packet loss events occurred during short periods, whereas most of the time the packet loss rate was minimal. During the same measurement period, we also used the active monitoring tool Hades [1, 7] to measure the packet loss rate between the same pairs of networks. Hades estimates the packet loss rate of a path by sending a burst of 9 packets with 30 ms offset every minute. In contrast to PcktLoss, Hades reported only 245 lost packets.

6   Conclusion

We presented the design and implementation of PcktLoss, a novel method for the accurate measurement of the packet loss faced by user traffic. Based on passive network monitoring, PcktLoss can measure the packet loss ratio of *individual* traffic flows, allowing to pinpoint loss events for specific classes of traffic. Our experimental evaluation and real-world deployment have shown that PcktLoss can precisely measure the packet loss rate even when monitoring multi-Gigabit traffic speeds.

In our future work, we plan to explore how to conveniently integrate checks for packet drops in the packet capturing cards for eliminating any reported packet loss due to temporary overload. We also plan to explore how to efficiently monitor the packet loss rate in the presence of IP fragmentation halfway into the monitored network path.

Acknowledgments

This work was supported in part by the IST project LOBSTER funded by the Europen Union under Contract No. 004336. The work of Alexandros Kapravelos, Michalis Poly-chronakis and Evangelos Markatos was also supported by the GSRT project Cyber-scope funded by the Greek Secretariat for Research and Technology under Contract No. PENED 03ED440. Alexandros Kapravelos, Michalis Polychronakis and Evangelos Markatos are also with the University of Crete.

References

1. Hades active delay evaluation system,
   `http://www-win.rrze.uni-erlangen.de/ippm/hades.html.en`
2. Adamns, A., Mahdavi, J., Mathis, M., Paxson, V.: Creating a scalable architecture for internet measurement. In: Proceedings of INET (1998)
3. Adamson, B.: The MGEN Toolset, `http://pf.itd.nrl.navy.mil/mgen`
4. Benko, P., Veres, A.: A Passive Method for Estimating End-to-End TCP Packet Loss. In: Proceedings of IEEE Globecom, pp. 2609–2613 (2002)
5. Bradner, S., McQuaid, J.: Benchmarking Methodology for Network Interconnect Devices. RFC 2544 (Informational) (March 1999), `http://www.ietf.org/rfc/rfc2544.txt`
6. Hemminger, S.: Network Emulation with NetEm. In: Proceedings of Linux Conf. Au. (2005)
7. Holleczeck, T.: Statistical analysis of IP performance metric in international research and educational networks (diploma thesis) (2008)
8. Ohta, S., Miyazaki, T.: Passive packet loss monitoring that employs the hash-based iden-tification technique. In: Ninth IFIP/IEEE International Symposium on Integrated Network Management (IM) (2005)
9. Papadogiannakis, A., Kapravelos, A., Polychronakis, M., Markatos, E.P., Ciuffoletti, A.: Pas-sive end-to-end packet loss estimation for grid traffic monitoring. In: Proceedings of the CoreGRID Integration Workshop, pp. 79–93 (2006)
10. Savage, S.: Sting: A TCP-based network measurement tool. In: USENIX Symposium on Internet Technologies and Systems, USITS (1999)
11. Sommers, J., Barford, P., Duffield, N., Ron, A.: Improving accuracy in end-to-end packet loss measurement. In: Proceedings of the ACM SIGCOMM 2005, pp. 157–168 (2005)
12. Ubik, S., Smotlacha, V., Trocha, S., Leinen, S., Jeliazkov, V., Friedl, A., Kramer, G.: Report on passive monitoring pilot, Deliverable MS.3.7.5 GN2 Project (September 2008)
13. Ubik, S., Friedl, A., Hotmar, S.: Quantification of traffic burstiness with mapi middleware (September 2008)

Inferring Queue State by Measuring Delay in a WiFi Network

David Malone, Douglas J Leith, and Ian Dangerfield

Hamilton Institute, NUI Maynooth

Abstract. Packet round trip time is a quantity that is easy to measure for end hosts and applications. In many wired networks, the round trip has been exploited for purposes such as congestion control and bandwidth measurement because of relatively simple relationships between buffer occupancy and drain time. In 802.11 networks, the buffer drain times show considerable variability due to the random nature of the MAC service. We examine some of the problems faced when using round-trip-time-based queue estimates in these networks, particularly in relation to congestion control.

1 Introduction

Network round-trip time is a useful measurement that is easily estimated by end hosts. It is often used as a measure of network congestion either implicitly (e.g. a human looking at the output from traceroute or ping) or explicitly (e.g. TCP Vegas [3], FAST [13] or Compound TCP [12] use RTT as a proxy measure of buffer occupancy). The assumption is that queueing is the main source of variation in RTTs, and so RTTs can be used to estimate queueing. This has led to tools such as pathchar [7].

In wired networks, this is often a reasonable assumption: there is usually a linear relationship between queue length and queue drain time. However, this relationship is not universal. In WiFi networks there can be a significant random component associated with transmitting packets. A device usually has a back-off period before sending. The duration of this period is a combination of a randomly selected number and the duration of busy periods due to other traffic on the network [6]. Also, a packet may suffer a collision or corruption, requiring further back-off periods and retransmission.

Figure 1 shows observed queue drain times plotted against queue length from a device transmitting packets over a contended WiFi link. A striking feature of this graph is the overlap between RTTs associated with different queue lengths: RTTs observed for a queue length of one packet could have come from a queue length of 10 packets; RTTs from a queue of 10 packets could easily have come from a queue of 20 packets. Even before other sources of delay are considered, this is a challenging environment for making inferences about queue length from RTTs.

Previous work has touched on the impact of this variability. A comparison of bandwidth estimation tools over wireless was conducted in [11]. They suggest that some errors made by bandwidth estimation tools may be due to variable service, but they do not conduct an in-depth investigation of this. Other work, such as [5] looks at various TCP metrics over WiFi. They consider RTT averaged over connection lifetimes, but are not concerned with the relationship between measured RTT and buffer occupancy.

M. Papadopouli, P. Owezarski, and A. Pras (Eds.): TMA 2009, LNCS 5537, pp. 8–16, 2009.

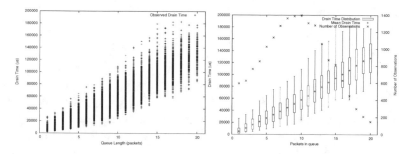

Fig. 1. Impact of Queue Length on Drain Time. (a) Scatter plot of observed values. (b) 10–90% box-and-whiskers plot and mean; number of samples is also shown on right hand axis.

In this paper we investigate the complications introduced by the random nature of the service in 802.11. We note that there have been complications in application or transport layer measurement of RTTs in wired networks (for example, some filtering is necessary to remove artifacts caused by TCP's delayed ACKing or TSO [8]). However, in order to focus on the issues raised by the varying delay of a wireless link, in this paper we will assume that accurate RTT measurements are available.

We show that raw RTT measurements don't allow sharp conclusions to be drawn about the queue length, but are well correlated with it. We also show that variability in measurements grows as $\sqrt{n}$. We then look at filters that might be applied to the RTT measurements and find that normal RTT filters *decrease* correlation. Linux's Vegas implementation deals relatively well with these challenges and we consider why this is.

2   Testbed Setup

We consider network delay associated with winning access to transmission opportunities in an 802.11 WLAN. We measure both the queue drain time (the time from when a packet reaches the driver to when the transmission is fully complete) and the MAC service time (the time from reaching the head of the hardware interface queue to when transmission is fully complete), using techniques described in [4]. The MAC service time can vary by orders of magnitude, depending on network conditions.

The 802.11 testbed is configured in infrastructure mode. It consists of a desktop PC acting as an access point, 15 PC-based embedded Linux boxes based on the Soekris net4801 [2] and one desktop PC acting as client stations. The PC acting as a client records measurements for each of its packets, but otherwise behaves as an ordinary client station. All systems are equipped with an Atheros 802.11b/g cards.

All nodes, including the AP, use a Linux kernel and a version of the MADWiFi [1] wireless driver modified to record packet statics at the driver layer with a fixed queue of 20 packets. While we focus on the queueing at the drive layer, Section 3 shows the statistics of drain time as the number of packets increases. All of the tests are performed using the 802.11b physical maximal transmission rate of 11Mbps with RTS/CTS disabled and the channel number explicitly set.

3   Raw RTT Signal

The data for Figure 1 is taken from a run from our testbed where 4 stations are uploading using TCP. Measurements are taken from one TCP sender, so all packets are 1500 bytes. The results are taken over about 110s where network conditions are essentially static.

Briefly consider the simple problem of determining if the queue in Figure 1 contains more than ten packets based on the observed drain time. For example, consider a simple threshold scheme: set a threshold and if the observed time is greater than the threshold, we infer it has more than ten packets, otherwise we infer it has less than ten packets. Even if we have prior knowledge of the drain time distribution in Figure 1, how effective can such a scheme be for WiFi?

Figure 2 shows how often this scheme makes a mistake for a range of different thresholds. The upper curve in Figure 2(a) is the chance that the delay threshold incorrectly indicated that the queue length was either above or below 10 packets. The upper curves in Figure 2(b) show how this breaks down into situations where the queue was small but the delay was big or the queue was big but the delay was small. The best choice of threshold, around $60,000\mu s$ (about 10 times the mean service time), makes a mistake just over 10% of the time. Thus a congestion control scheme based on such a threshold could make an incorrect decision about once in every ten packets.

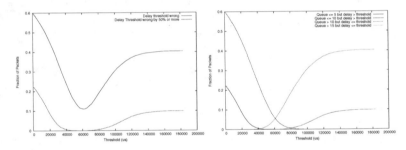

Fig. 2. Simple thresholding of delay measurements: (a) how often simple thresholding is wrong, (b) breakdown of errors into too big or too small

Of course, it is possible that these mistakes occur mainly when the queue is close to 10 packets. To check this we also calculate the chance that while the queue had five of fewer packets that the delay is less than the threshold and the chance that the queue has more than fifteen packets while the delay is short. These represent large mistakes by the threshold technique. The results are the lower set of curves in Figure 2(a), with a large flat section for threshold values from 40,000 to $80,000\mu s$. While it is making mistakes regularly these are not gross mistakes. A range of thresholds produce reasonable results.

This suggests that though delay measurements are quite noisy, there is hope of learning information about queue length from them. Basic statistics for the drain times against queue lengths are shown in Figure 1(b). We show the mean drain time and a box-and-whiskers plot showing the range and the 10th and 90th percentiles.

Figure 3(a) shows the estimated autocorrelation for the MAC service times, queue drain times and queue lengths. We see that the MAC service times show no evidence of

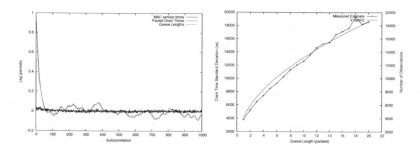

Fig. 3. Drain time statistics. (a) Autocorrelation for the sequence of MAC service times, queue drain times and queue lengths. (b) Estimate of standard deviation of drain times as a function of queue length.

correlation structure. This is what we intuitively expect from an 802.11 network operating without interference. In contrast, the queue lengths show a complicated correlation structure. The queue lengths are sampled at the time a transmission completes; because the queue length will not change much between these times we expect strong correlation over lags comparable to the queue length. The longer term structure in the queue length will be a function of TCP's congestion control behaviour in this network. Finally, the queue drain times show a *similar* structure to that observed for the queue lengths. This is encouraging: the drain time and the queue length are in a sense carrying similar information. We can confirm this by calculating the Pearson correlation value of 0.918.

Based on the low autocorrelation of the MAC service times, it may be reasonable to approximate the drain time of a queue of length n as the sum of n independent service times. The variance of the sum of random variables grows like the sum of the variances. Thus we expect the range of the 10–90% percentiles to scale like $\sqrt{n}$. This is confirmed in Figure 3(b), where we plot standard deviation of the drain times and compare them to $\sqrt{n}$. Larger buffers will make queue estimation even more challenging.

4   Smoothed RTT Signal

Most RTT measurements are smoothed before use, and based on the statistics we have seen in the previous section, there is a reasonable possibility that this may help in understanding queue behaviour. In this section we look at the impact of a number of commonly used filters on our ability to estimate the queue length.

A well-known example of the use of a smoothed RTT is the sRTT used in TCP to estimate round-trip timeouts. This estimator updates the smoothed estimate every time a new estimate arrives using the rule

$$\text{srtt} \leftarrow 7/8\text{srtt} + 1/8\text{rtt}. \tag{1}$$

We'll refer to this as 7/8 filter. It is also used in Compound TCP for delay based congestion control. We can do similar smoothing based on the time between packets:

$$\text{srtt} \leftarrow e^{-\Delta T/T_c}\text{srtt} + (1 - e^{-\Delta T/T_c})\text{rtt}. \tag{2}$$

ΔT is the time since the last packet and T_c is a time constant for the filter. This filter approximately decreases the weight of RTT estimates exponentially in the time since the RTT was observed. We'll refer to this as the Exponential Time filter.

TCP Vegas and derivatives use a different smoothing. Ns2's implementation of Vegas uses the mean of the RTT samples seen over a window of time that is about the same as the current RTT. In order to avoid spurious spikes due to delayed acking, the Linux implementation of Vegas uses the minimum of the RTT's seen over a similar window. We'll refer to these as the Windowed Mean and Windowed Minimum filters.

We applied these filters to the drain time data to see if the resulting smoothed measurement was a better predictor of the queue length. We used a window size/time constant of 100ms, which is comparable to the actual RTT in our experiment. The results of our simple threshold test and calculation of autocorrelation are shown in Figure 4.

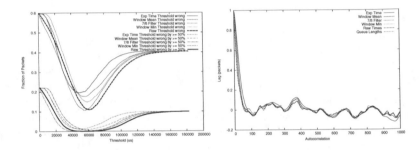

Fig. 4. Thresholding of filtered delay measurements: (a) errors while thresholding simple measurements, (b) autocorrelation of filtered measurements

Interestingly, the filters *except for* Windowed Minimum have made things worse. Achievable error rate for thresholding has increased from 11% to 15, 18 and 20% for 7/8s, Windowed Mean and Exponential Time filters. The Windowed Minimum achieves an error rate of around 10.5%, which is comparable with the raw drain time error rate.

The autocorrelation graph tells a similar story: raw times and Windowed Minimum follow the queue length most closely. The Windowed Minimum measurements have the highest Pearson correlation with the queue length (0.922) closely followed by the raw measurements (0.918). There is then a gap before the 7/8th filter, the Windowed Mean and the Exponential Time results (0.836, 0.797 and 0.752 respectively).

5   Variable Network Conditions

As noted, the length of 802.11's random backoff periods are not just based on the selection of a random number, but also on the duration of busy periods due to the transmissions of other stations. In addition, the number of backoff periods is dependent on the chance of a collision, which is strongly dependent on the number of stations in the network and their traffic. Thus the RTTs observed by a station depend on cross traffic that may not even pass through the same network buffers.

For example, consider Figure 5. This shows the time history of queue lengths and drain times as we shut down the competing stations from the setup described in Section 3. By 242s there is little competing traffic in the system, and Figure 5(a) shows that the mean drain time and variability have been radically reduced. However, if we look at Figure 5(b) we see that this is not because the queue size has been reduced. In fact TCP Reno is keeping the queue closer to full because of reduced RTTs and contention.

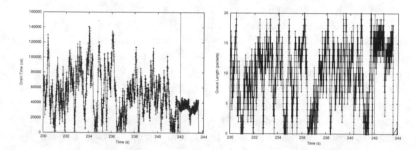

Fig. 5. The impact of other stations leaving the system: (a) drain times and (b) queue lengths

When stations join the system the impact can also be dramatic, as shown in Figure 6. 4 TCP uploads are joined by another 4 TCP uploads just after 120s (note, to get 8 TCP uploads to coexist in a WLAN, we have used the ACK prioritisation scheme from [9], resulting in smoother queue histories). We see basically no change in queue length, but almost a doubling of round trip time.

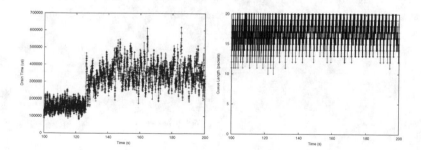

Fig. 6. The impact of other stations joining the system: (a) drain times and (b) queue lengths

These changes in drain time are caused by a change in the mean service rate for the queue. Clearly, any scheme for detecting queue length based on round-trip time would have detect changes in network conditions and re-calibrate. This also creates a problem for systems that aim to measure the base RTT, i.e. the round-trip time in the absence of queueing. Because the mean service rate depends on traffic that is not in the queue, a change in other traffic can cause a shift in the base RTT. As queueing time is usually estimated as RTT − baseRTT, this could be an issue for many schemes.

6 Impact on TCP Vegas

We now look at the performance of Linux's TCP Vegas in light of our observations. We consider Vegas because it is one of the simplest delay-based congestion control schemes. We expect other delay based schemes, such as FAST and Compound, to face similar challenges. Linux's Vegas module alters congestion avoidance behaviour but reverts to Reno-like behaviour in other situations. Over each cwnd's worth of packets it collects a minimum RTT observed over that cwnd. It also maintains a base RTT, which is the smallest cwnd observed over the current period of congestion avoidance.

The target cwnd is then estimated as cwnd × baseRTT/minRTT. The difference between this and the current cwnd is compared to the constants $\alpha = 2$ and $\beta = 4$. If the difference is less than α cwnd is increased, if it is greater than β it is decreased. Vegas aims to introduce a few packets more than the bandwidth-delay product into the network resulting in a small standing queue.

We anticipate two possible problems for Vegas. First, because Vegas is using RTT measurements, it is possible that the noise in these measurements will cause Vegas to incorrectly manage the queue, either resulting in an empty queue (reducing utilisation) or overfilling the queue (resulting in drops, which delay-based schemes aim to avoid). Second, after a change in network conditions, Vegas may use an incorrect baseRTT. If this change results in an increased baseRTT then Vegas might continually reduce cwnd in an attempt to reduce the observed minRTT, resulting in poor utilisation.

To investigate these potential issues, we run a TCP flow across our testbed with various round trip times introduced with Dummynet [10]. After 60s we change the network conditions by introducing additional 11 stations, one per second, sending UDP packets at a high rate. First, as a baseline, we run a set of experiments with very large buffers and TCP Reno. Reno keeps these buffers from emptying, and so gives an indication of the best achievable throughput. Results for Reno with a 5ms, 50ms and 200ms RTT are similar to the throughput for Vegas shown in Figure 7.

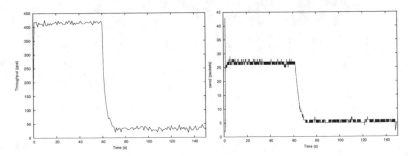

Fig. 7. Vegas with 5ms additional RTT in an initially uncontended WLAN with additional flows introduced around 60s: (a) throughput, (b) cwnd

Figure 7 shows throughput and cwnd histories for Vegas with a 5ms RTT (results for Vegas with a 50ms RTT are broadly similar). We observe that in terms of throughput, it compares well with Reno, both before and after the introduction of additional flows.

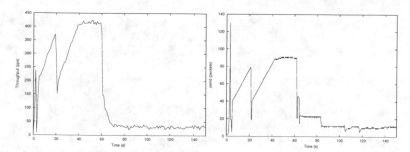

Fig. 8. Vegas with an additional 200ms RTT in an initially uncontended WLAN with additional flows introduced around 60s: (a) Throughput. (b) Cwnd.

Can we understand why Vegas does not keep reducing cwnd? If we calculate the min-RTT that is the threshold for increasing cwnd, we get a value of $\text{baseRTT}/(1 - \frac{\alpha}{\text{cwnd}})$. The upper threshold for decreasing cwnd is the same, but with β instead of α. When cwnd is small, the band for maintaining or increasing cwnd becomes larger. Thus, as cwnd becomes smaller Vegas can accommodate increased variability, though it may decrease cwnd below the bandwidth-delay product before this comes into play.

Figure 8 shows results for Vegas with a 200ms RTT. Vegas is behaving in a different way: it experiences losses even when not competing with other stations. This may be due to Vegas maintaining a longer queue, and consequently seeing larger fluctuations due to the random service. At 200ms the queue fluctuations are large enough that packets are lost, resulting in Vegas reverting to Reno until it re-enters congestion avoidance. This resets the baseRTT, allowing Vegas to recover when new flows are introduced.

7   Conclusion

In this paper we have studied a number of interesting problems faced when inferring buffer occupancy from RTT signals in a WiFi network. We have seen that the raw RTT signal is correlated with buffer occupancy, but there is significant noise that grows as buffer occupancy increases. Standard smoothing filters seem to reduce our prospects of estimating buffer size. We have also seen that traffic that does not share a buffer with our traffic may have a significant impact on the RTT measurements, possibly creating problems for estimation of queue length under changing network conditions. We have briefly looked at the implications of these observations for Linux's Vegas implementation. While Vegas performs well in our simple tests, possibly due to its use of a Windowed Minimum filter. We believe these observations will prove useful in designing delay-based congestion-control for WiFi.

References

1. Multiband Atheros driver for WiFi (MADWiFi) r1645 version,
   http://sourceforge.net/projects/madwifi/
2. Soekris engineering, http://www.soekris.com/

3. Brakmo, L., Peterson, L.: Tcp vegas: End to end congestion avoidance on a global internet. IEEE Journal on Selected Areas in Communication 13(8), 1465–1480 (1995)
4. Dangerfield, I., Malone, D., Leith, D.J.: Experimental evaluation of 802.11e EDCA for enhanced voice over WLAN performance. In: Proc. WiNMee (2006)
5. Franceschinis, M., Mellia, M., Meo, M., Munafo, M.: Measuring TCP over WiFi: A real case. In: WiNMee (April 2005)
6. IEEE. Wirless LAN Medium Access Control (MAC) and Physical Layer (PHY) Specifications, IEEE std 802.11-1997 edition (1997)
7. Jacobson, V.: Pathchar - a tool to infer characteristics of internet paths. MSRI (April 1997)
8. McCullagh, G.: Exploring delay-based tcp congestion control. Masters Thesis (2008)
9. Ng, A.C.H., Malone, D., Leith, D.J.: Experimental evaluation of TCP performance and fairness in an 802.11e test-bed. In: ACM SIGCOMM Workshops (2005)
10. Rizzo, L.: Dummynet: a simple approach to the evaluation of network protocols. ACM/SIGCOMM Computer Communication Review 27(1) (1997)
11. Sundaram, N., Conner, W.S., Rangarajan, A.: Estimation of bandwidth in bridged home networks. In: Proc. WiNMee (2007)
12. Tan, K., Song, J., Zhang, Q., Sridharan, M.: A compound tcp approach for high-speed and long distance networks. In: INFOCOM (2006)
13. Wei, D.X., Jin, C., Low, S.H., Hegde, S.: FAST TCP: motivation, architecture, algorithms, performance. IEEE/ACM Transactions on Networking 14, 1246–1259 (2006)

Network-Wide Measurements of TCP RTT in 3G

Peter Romirer-Maierhofer[1], Fabio Ricciato[1,3], Alessandro D'Alconzo[1],
Robert Franzan[1], and Wolfgang Karner[2]

[1] Forschungszentrum Telekommunikation Wien, Austria
[2] mobilkom austria AG
[3] Università del Salento, Italy
lastname@ftw.at

Abstract. In this study we present network-wide measurements of
Round-Trip-Time (RTT) from an operational 3G network, separately
for GPRS/EDGE and UMTS/HSxPA sections. The RTTs values are estimated from passive monitoring based on the timestamps of TCP handshaking packets. Compared to a previous study in 2004, the measured
RTT values have decreased considerably. We show that the network-wide
RTT percentiles in UMTS/HSxPA are very stable in time and largely
independent from the network load. Additionally, we present separate
RTT statistics for handsets and laptops, finding that they are very similar in UMTS/HSxPA. During the study we identified a problem with
the RTT measurement methodology — mostly affecting GPRS/EDGE
data — due to early retransmission of SYNACK packets by some popular
servers.

1 Motivations

Third-generation (3G) cellular networks provide wireless Internet access to a
growing population of mobile and nomadic users. Since the early deployment of
GPRS and UMTS at the beginning of this decade, operational 3G networks have
been continuously evolving. The introduction of EDGE and HSDPA/HSUPA
(or HSxPA) respectively in GPRS and UMTS has increased the available radio bandwidth, while further upgrades are promised by the next wave of radio technologies like HSPA+ and LTE — refer to [7] for more details on 3G
technology evolution. The combination of higher bandwidth and cheaper tariffs
has produced a substantial growth of 3G user population and traffic volumes
(see e.g. [9], which in turn led to major upgrades also in the Core Network. The
functional complexity and ever-evolving nature of the 3G infrastructure increase
its exposure to problems and errors. Therefore, it is compelling for 3G operators
to be able to readily detect network problems and anomalous incidents. To this
purpose the operators deploy a number of monitoring and alerting systems, each
covering a different section of the global infrastructure and relying on different
types of input data and sensors — both passive and active.

M. Papadopouli, P. Owezarski, and A. Pras (Eds.): TMA 2009, LNCS 5537, pp. 17–25, 2009.

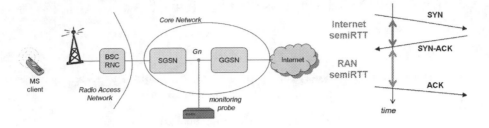

Fig. 1. Monitoring setting (left) and RTT computation scheme (right)

A class of anomaly sensors can be built upon the real-time analysis of packet-level traffic monitors. The basic idea is simple: extract a set of network performance indicators — we call them "network signals", e.g. delays percentiles or loss rate — out of the packet-level trace stream, and seek for deviations from the "normal" profile observed in the past. Such approach underlies two fundamental assumptions: (i) that network performances and the associated "signals" are stable under problem-free operation, and (ii) that network problems induce a recognizable deviation in at least a subset of the monitored network signals.

In this work we consider the possibility of using Round-Trip-Times (RTT) measurements, as obtained from passive analysis of TCP handshaking packets, as a possible "network signal" for detection of network anomalies. We present large-scale measurements from an operational 3G network and investigate the stability of the underlying distributions. Our results are based on very recent traces (January 2009) and include HSDPA/HSUPA and EDGE traffic.

The methodology of inferring RTT from passive TCP traces is not new. Benko et al. [1] reported large-scale measurements of TCP RTT from an operational GPRS network already in 2004. We adopt here the same methodology of [1] which considers exclusively SYN/ACK pairs, but provide results also for GPRS/EDGE and UMTS/HSxPA sections. Vacirca et al. [2] reported RTT measurements from an operational UMTS network, with data from 2004, considering also DATA/ACK packet pairs. Since then, the capacity of 3G network has increased considerably, due to the introduction of HSxPA and EDGE, and consequently the measured RTT values are now considerably lower. While some recent papers have investigated the delay process in HSDPA via active measurements (e.g. [3,4]), to the best of our knowledge this is the first study to report on large-scale passive measurement of RTT in a modern 3G network.

2   Measurement Setting

The measurement setting is depicted in Fig. 1. Packet-level traces are captured on the so-called "Gn interface" links between the SGSN and GGSN — for a detailed overview of the 3G Core Network structure refer to [5]. We use the METAWIN monitoring system developed in a previous research project and deployed in the network of a major mobile operator in EU — for more details

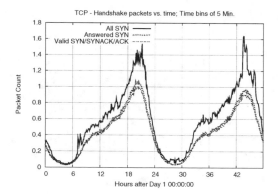

Fig. 2. Time-series of $N_{syn}(k)$, $N_{acked}(k)$ and $N_{valid}(k)$, 5 min bins (rescaled values)

refer to [6]. The monitoring system is able to extract IP packets from the lower 3GPP layers (GTP protol on Gn, see [5]) and discriminate the connections originated in the GPRS/EDGE and UMTS/HSxPA radio sections. In this study we provide network-wide measurements but in principle one can extract separate signals at finer spatial granularity, e.g. for individual SGSN areas or BSC/RNC areas.

The RTT measurement methodology works as follows (ref. Fig. 1). We consider only the TCP connection openings in uplink, i.e. initiated by the client Mobile Stations (MS), for all destination ports. We ignore the downlink connections opened by the Internet hosts — these are present due e.g. to peer-to-peer applications. The elapsed time between the SYN in uplink and the associated SYNACK in downlink is taken as an estimation of the (semi-)RTT in the wired part of the network, between the Gn link and the remote server in the Internet. Hereafter we refer to such quantity as "wired RTT". Similarly, the elapsed time between the SYNACK in downlink and the associated ACK in uplink is taken as an estimation of the (semi-)RTT in the Radio Access Network (RAN), between the Gn link and the Mobile Station. We shall refer to such quantity as "wireless RTT". We extract valid RTT samples only from unambiguous and correctly established 3-way handshakes, and discard all those cases where the association between packet pairs is ambiguous — e.g. due to retransmission, duplication, mismatching sequence number. All valid RTT samples within a measurement interval (e.g. 5 minutes or 1 hour) are aggregated into a logaritmically-binned empirical histogram. Additionally, for each measurement interval k we maintain three global counters: $N_{syn}(k)$ counts the total number of SYN observed in uplink, $N_{acked}(k)$ counts the number of SYN which received a SYNACK reply, finally $N_{valid}(k)$ counts the number of valid RTT samples after filtering out all ambiguous and incomplete sequences. The ratio $r_{inv} \triangleq 1 - \frac{N_{valid}}{N_{acked}}$ represents the fraction of invalid samples over the acknowledged SYN, i.e. the fraction of SYNACK packets that generate a valid RTT sample.

3   Measurement Results

In the following we present measurements taken in January 2009 from a subset
of Gn links (exact number undisclosed) of a nation-wide operational network
in Austria. Fig. 2 depicts the global counters $N_{syn}(k)$, $N_{acked}(k)$ and $N_{valid}(k)$
computed in 5 min intervals across two days. The values are rescaled in order to
hide the absolute volume of connections, as required by the non-disclosure policy
with the network operator. The time-of-day profile of network load achieves its
peak between 7-9pm, while at night it drops below 5% of the peak. The spikes in
the number of total SYN $N_{syn}(k)$ are due to some mobile stations occasionally
performing high-rate scanning.

3.1   Wireless Client-Side RTT

Fig. 3 plots the empirical Cumulative Distribution Function (CDF) of the wireless RTT separately for GPRS/EDGE and UMTS/HSxPA. Each graph includes
six curves for different measurement intervals of 1 hour each, at different time-
of-day. Both empirical distributions are considerably stable in time, with only
minor fluctuations between different measurement intervals. The upper tail of
the RTT distribution (ref. Fig 3) achieves values as high as a few seconds. Recall
from Fig. 1 that the wireless RTT values estimated by SYNACK/ACK pairs
include the delay components internal to the client terminal, e.g. packet processing time and I/O buffer delay. In some cases such internal components can
be very large. For example, the terminal I/O buffers can become congested due
to many paralallel downloads (self-congestion), for example in case of greedy
peer-to-peer file-sharing applications. Consider also that some mobile terminals
might have limited processing power and/or suboptimal implementation of the
TCP/IP stack. Besides terminal-internal causes, large delays can be due to *user
mobility*: if the client is moving to another radio cell the incoming downlink packets are buffered in the network — at the SGSN for GPRS/EDGE and at the RNC

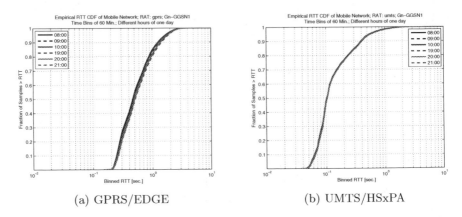

(a) GPRS/EDGE   (b) UMTS/HSxPA

Fig. 3. Empirical CDF of wireless client-side RTT, six intervals of 1 hour

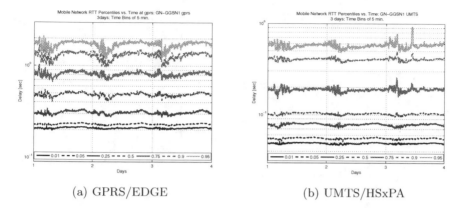

(a) GPRS/EDGE   (b) UMTS/HSxPA

Fig. 4. Percentiles of wireless client-side RTT, 5 min bins

for UMTS/HSxPA — until the handover is complete. Another possible source of delay for downlink packets are the *flow control* mechanisms implemented by the 3GPP stack to accommodate temporary dips in the radio channel bandwidth. In a previous study [8] on the same network we have observed that handovers and flow control jointly cause at least 5% of the downlink packets in GPRS/EDGE to remain buffered above 1 second in the SGSN.

Fig. 4 reports various RTT percentiles computed at 5 min granularity over three days, starting from 00:00 of Day 1. The lower 1%-percentile is around 50 ms in UMTS/HSxPA and 200 ms in GPRS/EDGE, while the median values are respectively at 100 ms and 500 ms. Recall that the median of GPRS RTT in 2004 was around 900 ms [1, Fig. 4]. The intervals of higher fluctuation in Fig. 4 correspond to night hours when the number of active MS and network load are very low, and so is the number of RTT samples per timebin.

To complete the overall picture we need to look at the ratio of invalid samples r_{inv}, which is plotted in Fig. 5(a) separately for the two radio technologies. The actual values are surprisingly high: for UMTS/HSxPA it is constantly around 4%, while for GPRS/EDGE it varies from 5% at night to 15% at peak hour. Such values were largely unexpected since we were assuming that the dominant cause for invalid client-side RTT SAMPLES is the loss of SYNACK packets in the RAN. Instead, after a deep exploration of the traces we discovered that the dominant cause is the early retransmission of SYNACK by some popular servers. More specifically, we identified over a hundred servers — all of them within the `google` domain — that were retransmitting the SYNACK packets after only 300-500 ms instead of the recommended timeout value of 3 seconds [10]. This causes an ambiguity when the RTT is larger than the retransmission timeout (see Fig. 5(b)) since the ACK replying to the first SYNACK will be seen after the second SYNACK. In this case it is not possible to associate univocally the ACK to one of the two SYNACK packets, leading to a case of ambiguity that is discarded as "invalid sample" by the current measurement methodology — the same as in [1]. Recalling from Fig. 3(a) that the value of 300 ms falls within

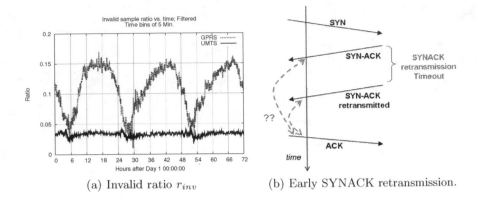

(a) Invalid ratio r_{inv} (b) Early SYNACK retransmission.

Fig. 5. Invalid ratio r_{inv} (a) and example of invalid RTT sample due to early SYNACK retransmission (b)

the range of client-side RTT values for GPRS/EDGE, and considering that a non-negligible fraction of connections are directed to `google` servers, it appears very likely that such high values of r_{inv} for GPRS/EDGE — and to a smaller extent also for UMTS/HSxPA — are due to this phenomenon. Clearly, this is introducing a bias into the RTT statistics, since for a certain share of the SYNACK (i.e. those sent by `google` servers) only the client-side RTT values that are smaller than 300 ms are recorded as valid samples, while the larger ones are discarded as invalid due to the duplicated SYNACK ambiguity.

In order to remove the bias on the RTT measurements we can follow two approaches. The simplest workaround is to ignore all SYNACK/ACK pairs coming from `google` servers, including the unambiguous ones, for example by filtering on the server-side IP address. This has the disadvantage of eliminating a non negligible part of the samples. More importantly, implementing such filtering would require to establish and maintain dynamically a list of filtered hosts, which is hurdle in practice. An alternative strategy would be to develop a method to resolve the duplicated SYNACK case, by inferring probabilistically which SYNACK to pick based for example on the RTT of other samples distribution. We leave the resolution of this problem as a point for further study.

Based on the presented results we can draw some conclusions for UMTS/HSxPA. We have seen that in the monitored network the performances of UMTS/HSxPA do not vary with the time-of-day (ref. to Fig. 4(b) and Fig. 5(a)), which means that they are poorly correlated with the network load. This indicates that the global network capacity is well provisioned. Instead for GPRS/EDGE we cannot draw any conclusion. Although it appears that some level of correlation with time-of-day is present for r_{inv}, this is not sufficient to quantify the degree of correlation between RTT and network load: in principle the daily profile of r_{inv} could be due differences in the traffic mix, and specifically in the relative share of traffic directed to `google`. More work is needed to resolve this issue.

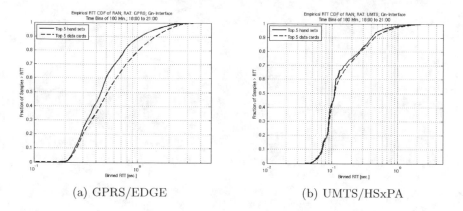

(a) GPRS/EDGE   (b) UMTS/HSxPA

Fig. 6. Distinct RTT statistics for handsets and laptops (top-5 TAC in each group)

One interesting feature of our monitoring system [6] is the ability to corre-
late information extracted at different 3GPP layers and on different interfaces.
Among other capabilities, the system is able to extract the Type Allocation
Code (TAC) contained in the International Mobile Equipment Identity (IMEI)
for each connection. Recall that the TAC identifies the terminal type, therefore
we can use such information to extract separate RTT measurements for each
class of terminal. In order to investigate whether there are differences between
the wireless client-side RTT profile for handsets and laptops, we have extracted
the top-5 TAC codes (ranked by the total number of valid RTT samples) for each
of these two classes of terminals, and we have computed the RTT statistics separately for each group. The resulting CDFs are given in Fig. 6. In UMTS/HSxPA
(Fig. 6(b)) the two distributions are very similar. Instead in GPRS/EDGE it
appears that handsets have *lower* client-side RTT than laptops. A first possible
explanation is that such difference is just an artifact due to the bias caused by
retransmitted SYNACKs: if the share of connections to `google` servers is different for laptop and handsets, also the impact of RTT bias will be different for the
two groups. A second alternative explanation is that handset users tend to generate less "aggressive" traffic than laptop users: for example, they tend to browse
one page at time instead of opening several parallel pages, avoid visiting heavy
websites, do not use peer-to-peer applications. Furthemore, many GPRS/EDGE
handsets use WAP. In other words, the traffic produced by individual handsets
tends to be smoother than laptops — shaped by applications and user behaviour
— therefore producing lower queuing delay on limited bandwidth links. At the
time of writing we are taking into consideration both hypotheses, and more
exploration of the data is needed to confirm or reject them.

3.2   Wired Server-Side RTT

For the sake of completeness we report in Fig. 7(a) the percentiles of the wired
RTT on the server side, for the whole traffic. The lower values in the range

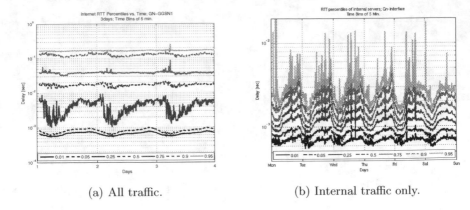

(a) All traffic.   (b) Internal traffic only.

Fig. 7. Percentiles of wired server-side RTT, 5 min bins

of a few milliseconds are partially due to connections terminated at operator's internal servers and proxies, located inside the Core Network, and partially to well-connected external servers, likely placed in the neighborhood of the peering links. It can be seen from Fig. 7(a) that the temporal profile of the 25%-percentile varies with the time-of-day, from 1-2 ms at night up to 6-8 ms in the peak hour. After further explorations we have found that this is due to variations of the external traffic mix, and specifically of the relative share of traffic directed to well-connected servers. In Fig. 7(b) we report the same percentiles only for the internal traffic, i.e. with SYNACK originated from the IP addressess internal to the CN domain. The RTT variations with time-of-day — hence with network load — are modest for the internal traffic, contained within 1-2 milliseconds, which indicates a relatively good provisioning of the internal servers.

4   Conclusions and Future Work

The results presented in this study confirm that modern 3G networks yield considerably lower RTT values than the initial GPRS deployment. We found that the network-wide performances — RTT distribution and invalid samples — are highly stable in time for UMTS/HSxPA, which indicates a negligible correlation with time-of-day and therefore a relative independence on network load. This is a first indication that the monitored UMTS/HSxPA network is currently very well provisioned. We have also shown that the global RTT distribution is essentially the same for handsets and laptops in UMTS/HSxPA.

During the study we have identified a limitation of the adopted RTT estimation methodology, namely the early retransmission of SYNACK packets after only 300 ms by some popular servers in the `google` domain. With the current methodology this leads to ambiguity in the RTT estimation and therefore to sample invalidation. The problem is present particularly on GPRS/EDGE, for which the typical RTT values are in the order of a few hundreds of milliseconds, where a non negligible fraction of samples are discarded. This leads to a bias in the RTT estimation which can not be quantified with our current data. In the progress of our work we intend to develop an effective method to solve the retransmitted SYNACK problem, either by probabilistic SYNACK resolution or by simple host-based filtering.

It is worth remarking that all presented time-series — RTT percentiles and invalid sample ratio — have pretty regular temporal profiles: flat or with regular daily cycles. This simplifies the task of detecting deviations in such signals that might reveal a network problem. On the other hand, it remains to be seen whether such signals can capture network anomalies, and of which kind. The present study could not address this aspect due to the absence of any network incident during the observation period. We are currently deploying on-line passive monitors in the operational network in order to collect long-term RTT measurements (weeks, months), so as to verify whether future network incidents are reflected in deviations of the network signals presented in this preliminary study.

References

1. Benko, P., Malicsko, G., Veres, A.: A Large-scale, Passive Analysis of End-to-End TCP Performance over GPRS. In: IEEE INFOCOM 2004 (2004)
2. Vacirca, F., Ricciato, F., Pilz, R.: Large-Scale RTT Measurements from an Operational UMTS/GPRS Network. In: Proc. of WICON 2005, Budapest (July 2005)
3. Jurvansuu, M., Prokkola, J., Hanski, M., Perälä, P.: HSDPA Performance in Live Networks. In: Proc. of IEEE ICC 2007, Glasgow (June 2007)
4. Barbuzzi, A., Ricciato, F., Boggia, G.: Discovering parameter setting in 3G networks via active measurements. IEEE Comm. Letters 12(10) (October 2008)
5. Bannister, J., Mather, P., Coope, S.: Convergence Technologies for 3G Networks: IP, UMTS, EGPRS and ATM. Wiley, Chichester (2004)
6. METAWIN and DARWIN projects: http://userver.ftw.at/~ricciato/darwin
7. Dahlman, E., Parkvall, S., Skold, J., Beming, P.: 3G Evolution: HSPA and LTE for Mobile Broadband, 2nd edn. Academic Press, Elsevier (2008)
8. Romirer-Maierhofer, P., Ricciato, F., Coluccia, A.: Explorative Analysis of One-way Delays in a Mobile 3G Network. In: IEEE LANMAN 2008, Cluj-Napoca, Romania (September 2008)
9. Heikkinen, M.V.J., Kivi, A., Verkasalo, H.: Measuring Mobile Peer-to-Peer Usage: Case Finland 2007. In: PAM 2009, Seoul (April 2009)
10. RFC 1122: Requirements for Internet Hosts — Communication Layers (October 1989)

Portscan Detection with Sampled NetFlow

Ignasi Paredes-Oliva, Pere Barlet-Ros, and Josep Solé-Pareta

Universitat Politècnica de Catalunya (UPC), Computer Architecture Dept.
Jordi Girona, 1-3 (Campus Nord D6), Barcelona 08034, Spain
{iparedes,pbarlet,pareta}@ac.upc.edu

Abstract. Sampling techniques are often used for traffic monitoring in high-speed links in order to avoid saturation of network resources. Although there is a wide existing research dealing with anomaly detection, few studies analyzed the impact of sampling on the performance of portscan detection algorithms. In this paper, we performed several experiments on two already existing portscan detection mechanisms to test whether they are robust enough to different sampling techniques. Unlike previous works, we found that flow sampling is not always better than packet sampling to continue detecting portscans reliably.

1 Introduction and Related Work

Traffic monitoring and analysis is essential for security and management tasks. In high-speeds links it is not always possible to process all the incoming packets and sampling techniques (e.g., Sampled NetFlow [1]) must be applied to reduce the load on routers. Robustness against sampling is very important since network operators tend to apply aggressive sampling rates when using NetFlow (e.g., 1/1000) in order to handle worst case scenarios. For this reason, it is fundamental to build sampling-resilient anomaly detection mechanisms.

We focus our study on portscan detection algorithms due to two main reasons. Firstly, they are one of the most common attacks (e.g., they usually precede worm propagation) and, therefore, there is general interest in detecting them reliably. Secondly, portscan attacks can put NetFlow-based monitoring platforms in serious trouble (the nature of this sort of anomalies can overflow flow tables due to the potentially large set of new flows generated by a scanner). Several methods for portscan detection exist. The most basic one flags a scanner when it connects to more than a certain number of destinations during a fixed interval of time. For example, this is the portscan detection algorithm implemented by the Snort IDS [2]. The mechanisms tested in this paper (TRW [3] and TAPS [4]) are more complex and have shown to be reasonably effective. In particular, TRW is implemented in the Bro IDS [5]. Few recent studies have analyzed the impact of sampling on anomaly detection [6,7,8]. Mai et al. studied the impact of packet sampling on TRW and TAPS in [6]. In the case of TRW, they found out that the flow size became lower in the presence of sampling, thus resulting in more false positives and negatives. They also showed that the metric used by TAPS is less affected, thus concluding that TAPS is more resilient to sampling than

M. Papadopouli, P. Owezarski, and A. Pras (Eds.): TMA 2009, LNCS 5537, pp. 26–33, 2009.

TRW. They also observed that, while TRW had better success ratio, TAPS exhibited a lower ratio of false positives. In [7], they tested packet sampling and three flow-based sampling mechanisms. They concluded that flow sampling was the best choice for anomaly detection under sampling. Finally, Brauckhoff et al. studied how specific metrics are affected by sampling looking at counts of bytes, packets and flows, together with feature entropy metrics [8]. They concluded that entropy summarization is more resilient to sampling than volume-based metrics.

In this study, we analyze the impact of sampling on TRW and TAPS portscan detection algorithms. In particular, we evaluated three sampling techniques: packet sampling, flow sampling and sample and hold. One of the main objectives of this paper is to validate previous results in our network scenario when using Sampled NetFlow data. We also aim to evaluate the impact of the different sampling techniques on portscan methods taking the same fraction of packets, while previous works (e.g., [7]) used instead the portion of sampled flows as the common metric to compare the different sampling methods. Although the amount of memory used by NetFlow to keep the flow tables is directly proportional to the number of flows, we focused on another relevant resource: the CPU cycles. Since in NetFlow every packet must be processed, it is also important to compare the accuracy of all sampling methods according to the ratio of sampled packets. The motivation of this study came from the fact that given a flow sampling rate, the fraction of analyzed packets is significantly different among the sampling methods, which results in an unfair comparison, specially for packet sampling. For instance, according to our traces, sampling 10% of flows results only in 2.86% of sampled packets, while flow sampling gets 10.90% and sample and hold takes even a larger proportion of packets (15.58%).

The rest of this paper is organised as follows. Section 2 presents the tested sampling methods together with the evaluated portscan detection algorithms. In Section 3, we describe our network scenario and the followed methodology. Section 4 shows and discusses the obtained results using real-world NetFlow data from a large university network. Finally, Section 5 concludes the paper and summarises our future work.

2 Background

In this section, we briefly describe the three sampling methods and the two portscan detection algorithms analyzed in this work.

2.1 Sampling Methods

We experimented with three different sampling methods: packet sampling (PS), flow sampling (FS) and sample and hold (SH). PS is widely used because of its low CPU consumption and memory requirements. Flow-based approaches (e.g., FS and SH) overcome some of the shortcomings of PS but, in exchange, they have higher resource requirements. Thus, some trade-off between accuracy and resource requirements is needed.

- **Random packet sampling** takes each packet with probability $p < 1$.
- **Random flow sampling** takes each flow with probability $p < 1$. This technique is usually implemented hashing the flow ID (e.g., the 5-tuple formed by the source and the destination IP addresses and ports, and protocol field). The flow is then selected if the resulting value (mapped to the [0..1] range) is below p [9].
- **Sample and Hold** takes the packet directly if its flow ID belongs to an already seen flow. Otherwise, the packet is sampled with probability $p < 1$. p is computed as $h \cdot s$ (s is the size of the packet and h is the probability of sampling a single byte) [10].

2.2 Portscan Detection Algorithms

Simple portscan detection algorithms, like the one used by the Snort IDS, are not very effective nowadays since attackers can easily evade detection by reducing their scanning rate. There are many other techniques capable of achieving higher rates of detection, such as TRW and TAPS, which we analyze in this paper.

- **Threshold Random Walk (TRW)** [3]. The main idea behind this technique is that one scanner will fail more connections than a legitimate client when trying to establish a connection. Since it is possible to fail some connections even being a good client, the decision of flagging a host as a scanner is not taken just after the first failure. For each source there is an accumulated ratio that is updated each time a flow ends. The update is done according to the flow state: connection established or failed attempt. We did our experiments with an unidirectional trace, so we used the proposed modification of TRW, called TRWSYN [4], that identifies a failed connection when an ended flow is a single SYN-packet. Eventually, if any source IP keeps scanning, it will fail more and more connections and finally it will exceed the established threshold, thus being recognised as a scanner.
- **Time-based Access Pattern Sequential hypothesis testing(TAPS)** [4]. This method is based on the observation that the ratio between the number of destination IPs and the number of destination ports (or the reverse) when the source IP is an scanner is significantly higher than the same ratio when there is no scanning activity. When this relationship is higher than a pre-configured threshold, the per-source IP ratio is updated accordingly. When this accumulated value reaches a certain limit, that source is considered to be a scanner.

3   Scenario and Methodology

We collected a 30-minute NetFlow traffic trace from the Gigabit access link of the Universitat Politècnica de Catalunya (UPC) (see Table 1 for more detailed information). This link connects about 10 campuses, 25 faculties and 40

Table 1. Detailed information about the NetFlow trace used in the evaluation and the absolute number of port scanners detected by TRW and TAPS

Date	Start time	Duration	Packets	Bytes	Flows	Total scanners	
						TRW	TAPS
06-11-2007	16:30	30min.	105.38×10^6	61.86×10^9	5.26×10^6	1457	4315

departments to the Internet through the Spanish Research and Education network (RedIRIS). Real-time statistics about the traffic of this link are available on-line at [11].

We first implemented the portscan detection techniques and the sampling methods described in Section 2 on the SMARTxAC monitoring system [12]. Then, we ran several tests with varying sampling rates, sampling methods and portscan detection algorithms. In order to have some ground of truth to check our results, we first ran each portscan detection algorithm without sampling (see Section 4 for more details about the used ground truth). After that, we can compare which attacks were missed in each case. We used the following sampling intervals $N = \{1, 10, 50, 100, 500, 1000\}$ to do our experiments.

We configured TRW and TAPS with a false positive ratio of 0.01, probability of detection to 0.99, probability of having a successful connection being a scanner to 0.2 and to 0.8 for a legitimate host as recommended by [3,4]. After some tests, we fixed the ratio used by TAPS to detect suspicious sources to $Z = 3$.

It is important to note that the sampling rate in the case of *PS* and flow-based sampling techniques has different meanings. While in the first case it refers to the fraction of sampled packets, in the latter case it indicates the portion of sampled flows. This results in a very different number of sampled packets and flows among the different sampling methods. In order to make all the sampling methods comparable, we used the following two metrics:

- **Equal portion of packets**. We first computed the packet sampling rate as $1/N$ for *PS*. Given this fraction of packets to keep, we then performed several tests to find the suitable sampling rates for the other sampling techniques in order to select the same portion of packets.
- **Equal portion of flows**. We computed the flow sampling rate as $1/N$ for *FS*. Given the portion of flows to take, we ran various tests to obtain the correct sampling rate values for *PS* and *SH* in order to sample the same portion of flows.

Tables 2 and 3 present the selected sampling rates that assure that the same portion of packets or flows is selected for all the sampling methods.

4   Performance Evaluation

In this section, we study the impact of *PS*, *FS* and *SH* sampling techniques on TRW and TAPS portscan detection algorithms. We used the following performance metrics:

Table 2. Percentage of selected flows given a portion of sampled packets

N	%packets	PS		FS		SH	
		p	%flows	p	%flows	h	%flows
10	10%	0.1	25.89%	0.092	10.24%	1.06×10^{-4}	6.84%
50	2%	0.02	7.95%	0.026	2.78%	2.8×10^{-5}	2.03%
100	1%	0.01	4.70%	0.015	1.85%	1.5×10^{-5}	1.05%
500	0.2%	0.002	1.44%	0.0036	0.95%	4×10^{-6}	0.53%
1000	0.1%	0.001	0.88%	0.0018	0.77%	2.7×10^{-6}	0.49%

Table 3. Percentage of selected packets given a portion of sampled flows

N	%flows	PS		FS		SH	
		p	%packets	p	%packets	h	%packets
10	10%	0.028	2.86%	0.1	10.90%	1.8×10^{-4}	15.58%
50	2%	0.003	0.33%	0.02	1.60%	2.8×10^{-5}	1.98%
100	1%	1.2×10^{-3}	0.12%	0.01	0.59%	1.5×10^{-5}	1.05%
500	0.2%	1.3×10^{-4}	0.013%	0.002	0.11%	9.511×10^{-7}	0.02%
1000	0.1%	6.2×10^{-5}	0.0062%	0.001	0.05%	9.456×10^{-7}	0.018%

$$success\_ratio = \frac{true\_scanners}{total\_scanners} \quad \text{and} \quad false\_positive\_ratio = \frac{false\_scanners}{total\_scanners},$$

where *total_scanners* accounts for our ground truth of scanners (scanners detected by TRW/TAPS without sampling, which are not necessarily real scanners). While *true_scanners* stands for the scanners detected under sampling that also belong to the ground truth, *false_scanners* refers to those detected scanners that fall out of that set. Note that our metrics differ from the classical definitions of success and false positive ratios in that we do not check whether the detected scanners by TRW and TAPS (without sampling) are real scanners or not. This choice lies in the fact that we are interested in evaluating the degradation of the portscan detection algorithms in the presence of sampling rather than in their actual detection accuracy. Table 1 presents the absolute number of portscans in our ground truth (i.e., without sampling).

We first focus on the impact of sampling on TRW. As we can observe in Figures 1(a) and 1(b), the success ratio degrades dramatically for increasing sampling rates regardless of the common metric being used (portion of packets or flows). When the sampling rate is low, TRW still detects few scanners but when it goes up, the success ratio reaches zero rapidly. Regarding the false positives ratio, Figure 1(d) shows that it is relatively low when using the same ratio of flows. When using the same proportion of packets (Figure 1(c)), we can notice that *PS* presents a huge peak that almost reaches 70%, while the flow-based sampling techniques hardly reach 10% of wrongly flagged scanners. As previously pointed out by former works, this peak for $N = 10$ is because of multi-packet flows converted to single SYN-packet flows, thus being flagged as scanners.

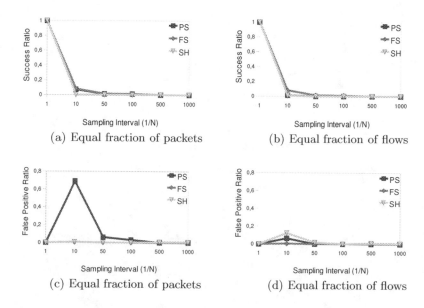

Fig. 1. Impact of sampling on TRW

When switching to TAPS and looking at the success ratio in Figures 2(a) and 2(b), we can observe that the obtained accuracy is very distinct among the three sampling mechanisms. When performing the experiment under the same fraction of packets, *PS* is clearly the best method, but when the common metric to compare is the ratio of flows, the accuracy is almost equal for all of them. Concerning to the false positives (Figures 2(c) and 2(d)), we observe that it is minimal ($< 2\%$) regardless of the sampling method and the common metric used.

The obtained results using the same fraction of flows showed lower values for both the success ratio and the false positive ratio than previous studies. The variation of the success ratio can be partly explained due to the different traffic traces used. Concerning to the false positive ratio (fpr), its decrease is related to the different followed methodologies. While [7] had approximately an initial $fpr = 0.75$ for their unsampled traces, we considered our ground truth to be classified without any erroneously flagged scanner ($fpr = 0$), thus focusing exclusively on the performance degradation due to sampling. While their fpr reached a ratio of almost 2.5, our maximum value is 0.12 (using the fraction of sampled flows to compare). When using the proportion of sampled packets as the common metric, this ratio increases to 0.7.

4.1   TRW vs. TAPS

As already noticed by previous studies, we were able to detect many more scanners using TAPS than TRW (see Table 1). This can be explained partially due to

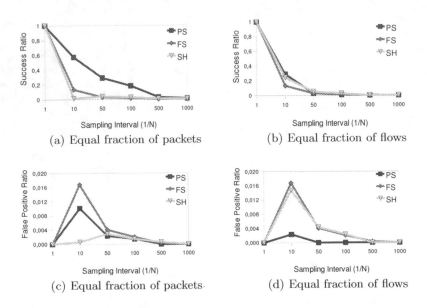

(a) Equal fraction of packets

(b) Equal fraction of flows

(c) Equal fraction of packets·

(d) Equal fraction of flows

Fig. 2. Impact of sampling on TAPS

the fact that TRW only works with TCP scanners and TAPS is connectionless-oriented. Furthermore, recent studies have observed that TRW tends to incorrectly detect P2P activity as scanners [13].

TRW showed to be much less resilient to sampling, while TAPS detected some scanners even for $N = 1000$. TAPS does not depend on any specific packet feature like TRW (which looks for single SYN-packet flows), thus being less sensitive to the particular packet discarded. TAPS also showed less false positives regardless of the common metric and the sampling method used, and it always got lower false positive ratios than TRW (the highest ratio showed by TAPS was 0.017 while TRW reached 0.7). Therefore, we can conclude that TAPS is better under sampling as already noticed by previous works. On the contrary, when using the same fraction of packets as the common metric to compare the different sampling methods under TAPS, we obtained better results using *PS* than flow-based techniques (*FS* and *SH*).

5   Conclusions and Future Work

In this paper, we have performed different experiments on TRW and TAPS to test whether they are robust enough to continue detecting portscans under sampling. Regarding the detection algorithms, we observed that TAPS is significantly better in the presence of sampling. Concerning to the sampling techniques, while flow sampling exhibited better performance than the rest using TRW, with TAPS we observed that packet sampling outperformed the flow-based mechanisms. The results presented in this paper are not entirely aligned with those obtained in former studies. In particular, it has been previously concluded that random flow sampling was always the most promising sampling method to detect portscans, but according to our results, we have not observed this superiority in all the experiments, thus confirming that this parallel study reveals new interesting information.

Our current work is centred in extending our study to other sampling methods and anomaly detection algorithms. We also plan to further validate the results of this work with more NetFlow traces from several networks.

Acknowledgements

This work was done under the framework of the *COST Action IC0703 "Data Traffic Monitoring and Analysis (TMA)"*. The authors thank UPCnet for the data traces provided for this study.

References

1. Cisco Systems: Sampled NetFlow,
   http://www.cisco.com/en/US/docs/ios/12_0s/feature/guide/12s_sanf.html
2. Roesch, M.: Snort–lightweight intrusion detection for networks. In: Proc. of USENIX Systems Administration Conference (1999)
3. Jung, J., Paxson, V., Berger, A., Balakrishnan, H.: Fast portscan detection using sequential hypothesis testing. In: Proc. of IEEE Symposium on Security and Privacy (2004)
4. Avinash, S., Ye, T., Supratik, B.: Connectionless portscan detection on the backbone. In: Proc. of IEEE International Performance Computing and Communications Conference (2006)
5. Paxson, V.: Bro: a system for detecting network intruders in real-time. Computer Networks 31(23-24) (1999)
6. Mai, J., Sridharan, A., Chuah, C., Zang, H., Ye, T.: Impact of packet sampling on portscan detection. IEEE Journal on Selected Areas in Communications 24(12) (2006)
7. Mai, J., Chuah, C., Sridharan, A., Ye, T., Zang, H.: Is sampled data sufficient for anomaly detection? In: Proc. of ACM SIGCOMM conference on Internet measurement (2006)
8. Brauckhoff, D., Tellenbach, B., Wagner, A., May, M., Lakhina, A.: Impact of packet sampling on anomaly detection metrics. In: Proc. of ACM SIGCOMM conference on Internet measurement (2006)
9. Duffield, N.: Sampling for passive internet measurement: A review. Statistical Science 19(3) (2004)
10. Estan, C., Varghese, G.: New directions in traffic measurement and accounting: focusing on the elephants, ignoring the mice. ACM Transactions on Computer Systems 21(3) (2003)
11. IST-Lobster sensor at UPC: http://loadshedding.ccaba.upc.edu/appmon
12. Barlet-Ros, P., Solé-Pareta, J., Barrantes, J., Codina, E., Domingo-Pascual, J.: SMARTxAC: a passive monitoring and analysis system for high-speed networks. Campus-Wide Information Systems 23(4) (2006)
13. Falletta, V., Ricciato, F.: Detecting scanners: empirical assessment on a 3G network. International Journal of Network Security 9(2) (2009)

Automated Detection of Load Changes in Large-Scale Networks

Felipe Mata, Javier Aracil, and Jose Luis García-Dorado

Universidad Autónoma de Madrid, Spain
{felipe.mata,javier.aracil,jl.garcia}@uam.es

Abstract. This paper presents a new online algorithm for automated detection of load changes, which provides statistical evidence of stationary changes in traffic load. To this end, we perform continuous measurements of the link load, then look for clusters in the dataset and finally apply the Behrens-Fisher hypothesis testing methodology. The algorithm serves to identify which links deviate from the typical load behavior. The rest of the links are considered normal and no intervention of the network manager is required. Due to the automated selection of abnormal links, the Operations Expenditure (OPEX) is reduced. The algorithm has been applied to a set of links in the Spanish National Research and Education Network (RedIRIS) showing good results.

Keywords: Load change, capacity planning, Behrens-Fisher problem.

1 Introduction and Problem Statement

The steady growth of Internet traffic [1,2,3] makes it necessary to pay close attention to load changes. Actually, network operators face bandwidth outages, and there is a growing pressure, both from customers and regulatory bodies, to ensure Quality of Service (QoS). Furthermore, operators are currently offering Service Level Agreements in their product portfolios, and the levels of QoS in terms of delay, bandwidth and jitter are very challenging to achieve in practice. Thus, there is an increasing need to detect changes in traffic load in order to perform an adequate capacity planning.

This paper focuses on detection of traffic changes in large-scale networks, i.e. with a very large number of links. In such networks, there are many traffic probes that produce time-series of link occupation (traffic volume). Being the number of links very large, it is not feasible to inspect all the time-series visually, and then make capacity planning decisions. The techniques provided in this paper allow the network manager to focus on those links that show a significant deviation from their typical behavior, and thus call for an upgrade.

On the other hand, we focus on the capacity planning timescale. The proposed detection techniques are amenable to use in the timescale of days or weeks. This is the timescale for capacity planning decisions ([4]), i.e. the timescale to decide whether more bandwidth should be rolled out and in which links. Therefore, this paper does not investigate the issue of reactive response in terms of severe traffic

M. Papadopouli, P. Owezarski, and A. Pras (Eds.): TMA 2009, LNCS 5537, pp. 34–41, 2009.

load peaks, which typically happens in the timescale of minutes or below. For this kind of traffic load detection a threshold-based algorithm applies better. On the contrary we focus on links with low-medium load that is increasing continuously over time. More specifically, we look for changes in traffic volume, which require intervention from the network manager, and possibly lead to a capacity planning decision.

The proposed technique employs a combination of clustering algorithms and the Behrens-Fisher test of hypothesis. The main advantage is that it reduces OPEX. Indeed, our technique marks the links as either remaining stable or changing in load and only the latter require human intervention. As a result, the load monitoring tasks are less time-consuming for the network manager.

Concerning the state of the art we find methods for traffic forecasting, such as the one presented in [5]. Our work provides a technique to decide if a link is deviating from its typical behavior but we do not perform traffic forecasting. The authors in [6] propose a model to decide when and to which capacity out of a discrete set is more convenient to upgrade a network link. The model takes into account economic variables such as the revenue, the risk free interest rate and the market price of risk to determine the value of the investment and based on these results the authors decide when is profitable to upgrade. Our work differs from this one because we detect the changes in load instead of running a model to check the network investment periodically. Our approach also diverges from the usual capacity planning studies where a link is marked as a candidate for upgrading when it does not met certain QoS metrics [7,8]. The difference is that our algorithm does not make the capacity planning decision by itself according to static thresholds, but it triggers a signal to a network manager to revise the logs and make the most convenient decision, based on the fact that a stationary load change has happened.

More related methods to our work are those presented in [9,10]. In [9] the authors make use of wavelets on attempts to detect changes in network measurements for the purpose of anomaly detection. The difference with our work is that we do not desire to detect anomalies (so we remove potentially anomaly data from our datasets, see Section 2) but to detect stationary changes in the network load, i.e. that the patterns of usage, the number of users, etc. have changed. On the other hand, [10] presents an adaptive sampling algorithm to enhance the traffic load measurements. This algorithm improves the results of load change detectors when applied to the measurement step, but does not introduce any novelty in the change detection mechanisms state of the art.

A brief description of our algorithm follows. First, clustering techniques are applied in order to find groups where the intra-group mean value is the same but the mean values between groups are different. To test whether the means are different or not, we apply the Behrens-Fisher methodology (we make no assumption about the covariance matrices), after testing that the data is indeed multivariate normal. The rest of the paper is structured as follows: Section 2 describes the dataset and Section 3 presents the methodology and addresses the main characteristics of the applied techniques. In Section 4 our online algorithm is described. Section 5 presents the results and Section 6 concludes the paper. Finally, future work is outlined in Section 7.

2 Data Set

We use MRTG [11] measurements from a set of links of the Spanish National Research and Education Network (NREN) RedIRIS[1]. We have collected MRTG logs for the traffic traversing the incoming and outgoing interfaces of several Points of Presence (POP) of the RedIRIS network. With a time granularity of five minutes, we have obtained 288 values for each day. In order to make this sample more manageable, we have averaged such values in 16 disjoint intervals of 90 minutes. The reasons to choose 90 minutes as the averaging period are manifold: first, there is a slim chance of missing data in the five minutes timescale, which is filtered out by averaging in 90 minute periods. Second, the time of the measurements may not be the same in the different POPs due to clock synchronization issues. A timescale of 90 minutes is coarse enough to circumvent this problem (this reason is also pointed out by [5]). Third, the assumption of normality for Internet traffic holds when there is enough temporal aggregation of the measurements [12,13]. Fourth, we require the day duration to be a exact multiple of the averaging period, in order to divide the days in the same intervals and track the daily pattern of network traffic. This daily pattern reflects intervals of high load in working hours and intervals of low load during night periods. Last, but not the least, there is a trade-off between a large averaging period, as required by the aforementioned reasons, and the precision obtained with a smaller one. We believe 90 minutes is a good compromise, which has also been adopted in other studies [5].

As we do not pursue to detect measurement anomalies, we remove potential abnormal data when preprocessing our dataset. Days where at least one of the 90 minutes intervals have no measurements are removed in order to avoid missing values in the dataset. Holidays and exam periods are also removed, since the measurements come from an educational network.

Note that this preprocessing can be performed on-line because these days are known in advance. Thus, the analyzer can be programmed with the days to be withdrawn from the traffic sample. Our measurements last from the 2nd of February 2007 to the 31st of May 2008. After the preprocessing step, the dataset contains more than 200 samples, each corresponding to a day worth of data that we model with a p-variate normal distribution, where $p = 16$ (16 periods of 90 minutes).

To facilitate the understanding of the relation of the number of the variable with the time period of the day to which it refers, these associations are presented in Table 1.

---

[1] http://www.rediris.es/

Table 1. Equivalence in time of the variables

Number of the variable	Time interval	Number of the variable	Time interval
1	00.00-01:30	9	12:00-13:30
2	01:30-03:00	10	13:30-15:00
3	03.00-04:30	11	15:00-16:30
4	04:30-06:00	12	16:30-18:00
5	06.00-07:30	13	18:00-19:30
6	07:30-09:00	14	19:30-21:00
7	09.00-10:30	15	21:00-22:30
8	10:30-12:00	16	22:30-00:00

3   Methodology

In this section we first present the clustering techniques that have been adopted and then provide a brief introduction to the Behrens-Fisher problem. The selected clustering algorithm was k-means[14], which is a two-step iterative algorithm that finds the clusters by minimizing the sum of the squared distances to a representative, which is called *centroid*. The input to the algorithm is the number of clusters k existing in the dataset (since we always look for two clusters, then $k = 2$). The choice of k-means for our online algorithm is due to the ease of adding a new instance to an existing model. To do this, it is only necessary to compute the distance from the new instance to the existing centroids, and then recompute the centroid for the cluster the new instance is assigned to. Finally, if the centroids have changed, k-means is applied again from a quasi-optimal solution, so the algorithm finds the new centroids faster than the first time. On the other hand, in order to obtain clusters that are adjacent in time (i.e. all samples sequential in time and not out of order) the UNIX initial time of the last sample of each day is included as an additional dimension.

To have statistical foundations that the obtained clusters in the former step are in fact different, we have applied the Generalized Behrens-Fisher Problem (GBFP). The GBFP is the statistical problem of testing whether the means of two normally distributed populations (X_1, X_2) are the same (null hypothesis H_0), for the case of unknown covariance matrices. The assumptions are that $X_i \sim \mathcal{N}_p(\mu_i, \Sigma_i), i = 1, 2$; i.e. the samples of population i come from a p-variate normal distribution with mean μ_i and covariance matrix Σ_i. To solve this problem the Hotelling's Generalized T^2-statistic is used, which is distributed as a central F-distribution under the null hypothesis of equality of means. When the sizes of the populations are not equal, a transformation is needed before computing the T^2-statistic (see Section 5.6 of [15]).

The GBFP assumes that the data comes from normal distributions. In order to trust in the results of the GBFP test, we have to make sure that our data is normal. To this end, we have performed several statistical tests to see whether the assumption of normality holds for each of the clusters. When testing for multivariate normality, it is necessary to perform tests for univariate normality of each of the dimensions, for bivariate normality in all the possible combinations of two dimensions and for p-variate normality (see for instance [16]). For univariate tests we have used Kolmogorov-Smirnov test, Lilliefors test and the Jarque-Bera test. For the multivariate tests we use the multivariate standard distance and χ^2 plots. Although it is necessary to test the normality assumption before each application of the GBFP test, these tests are lightweight and can be performed on-line very fast. If the normality condition does not hold, the distribution of the T^2-statistic under the null hypothesis may differ from the central F-distribution, and thus the probability of rejecting the null hypothesis when it is actually true would be different (Type I error).

4   Online Algorithm

The flux diagram of our algorithm is depicted in Fig. 1. First, daily traffic is collected (16 samples averaging each one 90 minutes of MRTG data) and the timestamp of the day is added (as the dimension 17), giving raise to a time-series of 17-dimensional vectors, where the first 16 dimensions are assumed to come from a 16-variate normal distribution. Then, clustering is applied to the time-series. If the number of samples per cluster is not enough to apply the

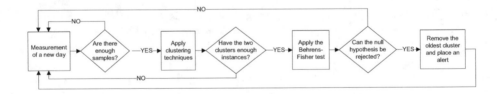

Fig. 1. Flux diagram of the online algorithm

GBPF (less than 17 samples per cluster [15]) we wait for a new day worth of measurements. When both clusters have enough instances, we test for normality and apply the GBFP to the resulting clusters if the normality assumption cannot be rejected. If the GBFP test determines that the null hypothesis of equality of means cannot be rejected, we mark the link as stable and wait for a new day worth of measurements, repeating the process. When the GBFP test shows statistical evidence of a difference in the means at a given significance level α, an alert is sent to the network manager. After the manager is alerted about the possible change in the means, we remove the oldest cluster from the dataset being analyzed and start the algorithm with the newest cluster as input. The results of applying our algorithm to real network measurements are presented in the following section.

5   Results

In this section we present the results of applying our methodology to the measurements of seven links in the RedIRIS network. Table 2 summarizes the number of tests performed and alerts generated. The second and fourth columns show the number of times the Behrens-Fisher testing methodology is applied. This is the number of times that the clustering algorithm was able to form two clusters with enough size to apply the test and the normality assumption held for both sets. It is worth mentioning that the null hypothesis of normality could not be rejected at the significance level $\alpha = 0.05$ for none of the obtained clusters. This supports our initial assumptions about the chosen averaging period (note also that the averaging process reinforces the supposition thanks to the Central Limit Theorem [17]). The third and fifth columns show the number of times an alert signal is sent, i.e. the null hypothesis of equality of means is not verified (again with $\alpha = 0.05$).

Table 2. Results for the online algorithm

University link	Incoming direction		Outgoing direction	
	Number of tests	Number of alerts	Number of tests	Number of alerts
U1	18	9	13	9
U2	13	9	14	7
U3	17	8	12	8
U4	15	8	20	7
U5	13	8	17	9
U6	15	7	11	8
U7	28	8	20	7

As can be seen in Table 2, the main advantage of our online algorithm to network load detection is the reduction in human interventions. This leads to a decrease in the OPEX costs making the network operator save money. The reduction of the human interventions is achieved because our algorithm produces an alert only in case a stationary statistically evident change in the load happens. The rest of the time the link is considered normal, and no intervention from the network manager is required.

Considering the time span of the measurements, our algorithm placed less than 10 alerts (potential network load changes) requiring human supervision in a period of more than 450 days (including holidays). That means a potential stable period between load changes of more than 45 days in average. To illustrate these results, Fig. 2 shows a time-series representation of the obtained groups with statistical evidence of different means. The data showed in that figure refers to the incoming direction of university link U1 for the time interval 12:00-13:30 (Variable 9).

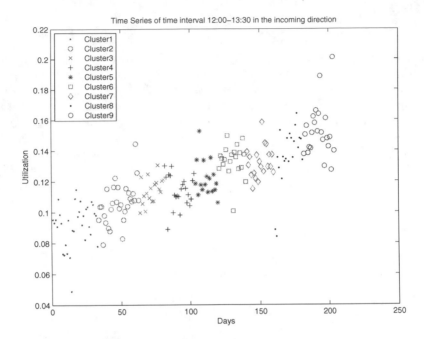

Fig. 2. Time-series plot for time interval 12:00-13:30 showing the different clusters found in the incoming direction of university U1

6   Conclusions

We have presented a new online algorithm for automated detection of network load changes, which has been applied to the Spanish NREN case. The algorithm makes use of well-known statistical techniques to reduce human intervention in network operation. This reduction is achieved by alerting the network manager only when there is statistical evidence of a change in the load, avoiding visual daily inspection of the load graphics for every link in the network. Finally, the capacity planning decision is deferred to the manager supervising the network.

7   Future Work

Several interesting issues remain open for further study. On the one hand, our approach uses a volume model of the network load. It would be interesting to take into account external variables as user demand or access capacity to develop more complex models that increase the accuracy of the detection trigger. On the other hand, it is important to know what limitations introduce the normality assumption and how to cope with them. In this light it would be interesting to know whether the traffic could be modeled with another kind of distribution, maybe using different larger timescales, and in those cases what would be the distribution of the statistic to test for differences in the means.

Acknowledgments. The authors would like to thank the anonymous reviewers for their valuable comments and to acknowledge the support of the Spanish Ministerio de Ciencia e Innovación (MICINN) to this work, under project DIOR (S-0505/TIC/000251).

References

1. Roberts, L.G.: Beyond moore's law: Internet growth trends. Computer (2000)
2. Paxson, V.: Growth trends in wide-area tcp connections. IEEE Network 8(4), 8–17 (1994)
3. Odlyzko, A.M.: Internet traffic growth: sources and implications. In: Proceedings of SPIE, vol. 5247, pp. 1–15 (2003)
4. Pióro, M., Medhi, D.: Routing, Flow, and Capacity Design in Communication and Computer Networks. Morgan Kaufmann Publishers Inc., San Francisco (2004)
5. Papagiannaki, K., Taft, N., Zhang, Z., Diot, C.: Long-term forecasting of Internet backbone traffic. IEEE Transactions on Neural Networks 16(5), 1110–1124 (2005)
6. D'Halluin, Y., Forsyth, P.A., Vetzal, K.R.: Managing capacity for telecommunications networks under uncertainty. IEEE/ACM Transactions on Networking 10(4), 579–588 (2002)
7. Fraleigh, C., Tobagi, F., Diot, C.: Provisioning IP backbone networks to support latency sensitive traffic. In: Twenty-Second Annual Joint Conference of the IEEE Computer and Communications Societies, INFOCOM 2003, vol. 1 (2003)
8. van den Berg, H., Mandjes, M., van de Meent, R., Pras, A., Roijers, F., Venemans, P.: QoS-aware bandwidth provisioning for IP network links. Computer Networks 50(5), 631–647 (2006)
9. Kyriakopoulos, K.G., Parish, D.J.: Automated detection of changes in computer network measurements using wavelets. In: Proceedings of 16th International Conference on Computer Communications and Networks (ICCCN), pp. 1223–1227 (2007)
10. Choi, B., Park, J., Zhang, Z.: Adaptive random sampling for load change detection. In: Proceedings of the 2002 ACM SIGMETRICS international conference on Measurement and modeling of computer systems, pp. 272–273. ACM, New York (2002)
11. Oetiker, T., Rand, D.: MRTG-The Multi Router Traffic Grapher. In: Proceedings of the 12th USENIX conference on System administration, pp. 141–148 (1998)
12. Kilpi, J., Norros, I.: Testing the Gaussian approximation of aggregate traffic. In: Proceedings of the 2nd ACM SIGCOMM Workshop on Internet measurment, pp. 49–61 (2002)
13. van de Meent, R., Mandjes, M.R.H., Pras, A.: Gaussian traffic everywhere? In: Proceedings of IEEE International Conference on Communications (ICC), Istanbul, Turkey, vol. 2, pp. 573–578 (2006)
14. Duda, R.O., Hart, P.E., Stork, D.G.: Pattern classification. Wiley, New York (2001)
15. Anderson, T.W., Wilbur, T.: An introduction to multivariate statistical analysis. Wiley, New York (1958)
16. Johnson, R.A., Wichern, D.W.: Applied multivariate statistical analysis. Prentice-Hall International Editions (1992)
17. Durrett, R.: Probability: Theory and Examples. Duxbury Press, Boston (2004)

Passive, Streaming Inference of TCP Connection Structure for Network Server Management

Jeff Terrell[1], Kevin Jeffay[1], F. Donelson Smith[1], Jim Gogan[2], and Joni Keller[2]

[1] Department of Computer Science
[2] ITS Communication Technologies
University of North Carolina
Chapel Hill, NC 27599
{jsterrel,jeffay,smithfd}@cs.unc.edu, {gogan,hope}@email.unc.edu

Abstract. We have developed a means of understanding the performance of servers in a network based on a real-time analysis of passively measured network traffic. TCP and IP headers are continuously collected and processed in a streaming fashion to first reveal the application-layer structure of all client/server dialogs ongoing in the network. Next, the representation of these dialogs are further processed to extract performance data such as response times of request-response exchanges for all servers. These data are then compared against archived historical distributions for each server to detect performance anomalies. Once found, these anomalies can be reported to server administrators for investigation.

Our method uncovers nontrivial performance anomalies in arbitrary servers with no instrumentation of the server nor even knowledge of the server's function or configuration. Moreover, the entire process is completely transparent to servers and clients. We present the design of the tools used to perform this analysis, as well as a case study of the use of this method to uncover a significant performance anomaly in a UNC web portal.

1 Introduction

Monitoring the performance of servers in a network is a challenging and potentially expensive problem. Common approaches are to purchase and install monitoring software on the server, or to use an active monitoring system that generates service requests periodically and measures the response time. Both approaches, while effective, typically require extensive customization to work with the specific server/service at hand.

We are developing an alternate approach based on passive collection of packet header traces, and real-time analysis of the data to automatically construct an empirical model of the requests received by servers and the responses generated. These models can be constructed for arbitrary servers with no knowledge of the functions performed by the server or the protocols used by the server. Given these models, we can easily compute important performance measures such as the response times for a server. Using statistical methods originally developed for medical image processing, distributions of these variables can be

M. Papadopouli, P. Owezarski, and A. Pras (Eds.): TMA 2009, LNCS 5537, pp. 42–53, 2009.

compared to archived historical distributions for each server to detect performance anomalies.

The approach works for arbitrary servers because it relies solely on properties
of TCP. Using knowledge of the TCP protocol, packet header traces (consisting of only TCP/IP headers and no application layer headers or payloads) are
processed in a streaming fashion to construct a structural model of the application dialog between each server and each client in real-time. This model is
an abstract representation of the pattern of application-data-unit (ADU) exchanges that a client and server engaged in at the operating system's socket
interface. For example, if a web browser made a particular request to a web
server that was 200 bytes long, and the server generated a response of 12,000
bytes, then by analyzing the headers of the sequence of TCP/IP packets flowing
between the client and server, we would infer this request/response structure
and represent this dialog as consisting of a single exchange wherein 200 bytes
were sent from client to server and 12,000 bytes were sent from server to client.
We intentionally ignore transport-layer effects such as segmentation, retransmission, etc. The model can be augmented to include both server-side and client-
side "think times" which can be inferred from the arrival time of the packets.
We refer to the server-side think times as *response times*, and they are our pri-
mary performance metric.

Using off-the-shelf hardware, we have constructed a network monitoring server
that is capable of tracing the 1 Gbps link connecting the 40,000 person UNC
campus to its upstream ISP, and performing the above analysis continuously,
in real-time, for all servers on the UNC campus. We have been continuously
tracing the UNC campus and gathering response time performance data for all
servers for a period of over six months. During this period we have processed
approximately 70 terabytes of packet headers. However, because our representation of client/server dialogs is relatively compact, the complete activity of the
UNC servers during this 6-month period requires only 3 terabytes of storage
(600 gigabytes, compressed). By mining these data for performance anomalies,
we were able to discover a significant performance anomaly that occurred to a
major UNC web portal. Over a period of three days in April 2008, the server
experienced a performance issue in which the average response time increased
by 1,500%. This discovery was made without any instrumentation of the server
or even a priori knowledge of the server's existence.

In this paper we present an overview of our method of capturing and modeling client/server dialogs and its validation. The dialogs are represented using
a format we call an *a-b-t connection vector* where a represents a request size,
b represents a response size, and t represents a think time. We present the an
overview of a tool we have developed called adudump that processes TCP/IP
packet header traces in real-time to generate *a-b-t* connection vectors for all
client/server connections present in the network. We then present some results
from an on-going case study of the use of adudump to generate connection vectors

for servers on the UNC campus network and the mining of these data to understand server performance. The tools used in this study and the data obtained will be publicly available for non-commercial use.

2 Related Work

Inferring the behavior of applications from analyses of underlying protocols is not new. For example, several schemes for monitoring web systems via an analysis of HTTP messages have been reported. Feldmann's BLT system [1] passively extracts important HTTP information from a TCP stream, but, unlike our approach, BLT is an off-line method that requires multiple processing passes and fundamentally requires information in the TCP payload (i.e., HTTP headers). This approach cannot be used for continuous monitoring or monitoring when traffic is encrypted. In [2] and [3], Olshefski *et al* introduce ksniffer and its improved sibling, RLM, which passively infer application-level response times for HTTP in a streaming fashion. However, both systems require access to HTTP headers, making them unsuitable for encrypted traffic. Furthermore, these approaches are not purely passive. ksniffer requires a kernel module installed on the server system, and RLM places an active processing system in the network path of the server. In contrast, our methods will work for any application-layer protocol and we can monitor a large collection of arbitrary servers simultaneously.

Commercial products that measure and manage the performance of servers include the OPNET ACE system[1]. ACE also monitors response times of network services but requires an extensive deployment of measurement infrastructure throughout the network, on clients, servers, and points in between. Fluke's Visual Performance Manager[2] is similar and also requires extensive configuration and integration. Also similar is Computer Associates Wily Customer Experience Manager[3]. CEM monitors the performance of a particular web server, and in the case of HTTPS, it requires knowledge of server encryption keys in order to function.

3 Measurement

The `adudump` tool generates a model of ADU exchanges for each TCP connection seen in the network. The design of the tool is based on earlier approaches for passive inference of application-level behavior from TCP headers (Smith *et al* [4], Weigle *et al* [5], Hernandez-Campos *et al* [6,7]). However, while these approaches build application-level models from packet headers in an offline manner, we have extended these techniques to enable *online* (real-time) inference (*i.e.* analyzing

---

[1] http://www.opnet.com/solutions/application_performance/ace.html
[2] http://www.flukenetworks.com/fnet/en-us/products/
    Visual+Performance+Manager/Overview.htm
[3] http://www.ca.com/us/performance-monitoring.aspx

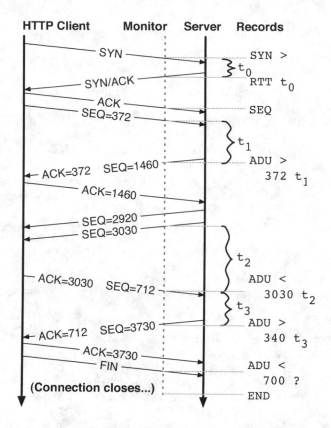

Fig. 1. *a-b-t* inference example

packets as they are seen at a monitor in a single pass). This affords the capability for *continuous* measurement of application-level data.

For a given connection, the core inference method is based on an analysis of TCP sequence numbers. As explained in [4,5], sequence numbers provide enough information to reconstruct the application-level dialogue between two end points. Figure 1 details the inferences that adudump draws for an example connection. adudump not only reports the size of the ADUs, but the application-level *think-time* between ADUs. A variety of contextual information is also printed, as shown in Table 1. Table 2 also gives an example of the data format.

To understand the inference, consider Figure 1. The connection "begins" when the three-way handshake completes. This event is marked with a SEQ record. The monitor sees a data segment sent from the client (in this case a web browser) to the server and makes a note of the time it was sent. The next segment is another data segment, sent in the opposite direction and acknowledging the previous data. Thus, adudump infers that the previous ADU (of 372 bytes) is completed, and generates a record with the ADU's size, direction, and subsequent think-time. The next segment, a pure acknowledgement (i.e. a segment without a

Table 1. The types of records output by `adudump`

Type	Information	Description
SYN	t, x, y, d	the initial SYN packet was seen at time t in direction d between host/port x and host/port y; connection-tracking state established
RTT	t, x, y, d, r	the SYN-ACK packet seen and round-trip-time measurement r
SEQ	t, x, y, d	the connection establishment
CONC	t, x, y, d	the connection has been determined to be concurrent
ADU	t, x, y, d, b, T	an application-level data unit was seen of size b bytes, and there was a think-time afterwards of T seconds. (The think-time is not always available.)
INC	t, x, y, d	report an ADU in progress (e.g. when input is exhausted)
END	t, x, y, d	the connection is closed; connection-tracking state destroyed

Table 2. `adudump` output format for an example connection. IP addresses (but not ports) have been anonymized.

```
SYN: 1202706002.650917 1.2.3.4.443 < 5.6.7.8.62015
SEQ: 1202706002.681395 1.2.3.4.443 < 5.6.7.8.62015
ADU: 1202706002.688748 1.2.3.4.443 < 5.6.7.8.62015 163 SEQ 0.000542
ADU: 1202706002.733813 1.2.3.4.443 > 5.6.7.8.62015 2886 SEQ 0.045041
ADU: 1202706002.738254 1.2.3.4.443 < 5.6.7.8.62015 198 SEQ 0.004441
ADU: 1202706002.801408 1.2.3.4.443 > 5.6.7.8.62015 59 SEQ
END: 1202706002.821701 1.2.3.4.443 < 5.6.7.8.62015
```

payload) is not used in determining ADU boundaries. In general, `adudump` ignores pure acks. Next, the server continues its response. Again, note that `adudump` generates no record until it infers that the ADU is complete. Also, note that the think-times that `adudump` reports are relative to the position of the monitor in the network. In other words, the think-times necessarily include a component of network delay as well. This is discussed in more detail in Section 4.

Note that this simple example assumes that the client and server take turns sending data. Such cases are called "sequential connections." "Concurrent connections," wherein both endpoints transmit simultaneously, can also be analyzed. Examples of such applications that employ concurrent connections include HTTP with pipelining enabled, peer-to-peer applications such as BitTorrent, and most interactive applications such as the secure shell. Connections are assumed to be sequential (i.e. non-concurrent) by default, until concurrency is detected by the existence of unacknowledged data in both directions simultaneously. Although concurrent applications do have a think-time, it is not possible to unambiguously determine the think-time without instrumenting the application. In our data,

ADUs from concurrent connections constitute approximately 5% of the connections, 25% of the ADUs seen, and 30% of the size in bytes.

4   Data

We have used adudump to generate a six-month data set of records of all TCP connections entering the UNC campus from the Internet, which we will make available through DatCat[4]. It is this data set that we will use for the remainder of this paper. Overall, we collected over three terabytes of data, modeling about 4 billion connections. Table 3 lists the individual collections, which were punctuated by measurement faults such as power outages and full disks. The records were captured by running adudump on a fiber split of the 1 Gbps link between the University of North Carolina and its commodity Internet uplink. Both directions of the link were tapped and fed to a machine with a 1.8 GHz Intel Xeon processor, 1.25 GB of RAM, and an Endace DAG card for packet capture. For privacy reasons, only inbound connections (*i.e.* those for which the initial SYN was sent to the UNC network) were captured. The collection process experienced very infrequent bouts of packet drops; the relatively old machine was able to keep up even when the link burst to its full 1 Gbps capacity.

Table 3. Data collection. All times local (EDT); all dates 2008. Data for Monday, March 17, was lost. Days are in MM/DD format. Durations are listed as days:hours:minutes.

#	begin	end	duration	outage	size	records	ADUs	conns
1	Fr 03/14 22:25	Th 04/17 03:50	33:05:25	1:14:11	813 GB	11.8 B	8.8 B	820 M
2	Fr 04/18 18:01	We 04/23 07:39	4:13:37	0:03:35	106 GB	1.6 B	1.1 B	116 M
3	We 04/23 11:14	Th 04/24 03:00	0:15:46	0:07:38	16 GB	234 M	161 M	19 M
4	Th 04/24 10:38	Fr 05/16 11:19	22:00:41	0:07:04	530 GB	7.7 B	5.7 B	532 M
5	Fr 05/16 18:23	Fr 05/23 00:06	6:05:43	5:16:20	108 GB	1.6 B	1.07 B	148 M
6	We 05/28 16:26	Mo 06/30 16:45	33:00:19	2:20:57	482 GB	7.3 B	4.7 B	686 M
7	Th 07/03 13:42	Fr 08/01 07:07	28:17:25	0:00:10	361 GB	5.7 B	3.5 B	563 M
8	Fr 08/01 07:17	Tu 08/19 13:12	18:05:55	1:02:05	273 GB	4.1 B	2.7 B	346 M
9	We 08/20 15:17	Mo 09/01 22:36	12:07:19	0:21:15	242 GB	3.6 B	2.5 B	271 M
10	Tu 09/02 19:51	We 10/01 21:25	29:01:34	n/a	629 GB	9.2 B	6.5 B	697 M
*			188:01:44	7:04:55	3.53 TB	52.8 B	36.7 B	4.2 B

Think-times reported by adudump are with respect to the monitor's vantage point, and think-times include an unknown component of network delay. However, note that since our monitor is at the edge of the UNC network, it is relatively close to the UNC servers. Since the UNC network is generally well-provisioned and well-designed, it is rare to see a intra-campus round-trip-time of more than a millisecond. For this reason, we only consider server-side think-times for the analysis, as these can be accurately inferred from our monitoring vantage point.

---

[4] http://imdc.datcat.org/

5 Validation

The heuristics that `adudump` uses to infer TCP connection structure are complex. Therefore, it is important to validate the correctness of `adudump` against a "ground truth" knowledge of application behaviors. Unfortunately, doing so would require instrumentation of application programs. As this is not feasible, we instead constructed a set of *synthetic applications* to generate and send/receive ADUs with interspersed think times.

To create stress cases for exercising `adudump`, the following were randomly generated from uniform distributions (defined by runtime parameters for minimum and maximum values) each time they were used in the application: number of ADUs in a connection, ADU sizes, inter-ADU think times, socket read/write lengths, and socket inter-read/write delays. There was no attempt to create a "realistic" application, just one that would create a random sample of plausible application-level behaviors that would exercise the `adudump` heuristics. The generated ADU sizes and inter-ADU think times as recorded by the synthetic applications comprise the ground truth, or the *actual* data. These synthetic applications were run on both sides of a monitored network link. We captured the packets traversing the link, saving the trace as a pcap file which we then fed as input to `adudump`, producing the *measured* data.[5] In this way, we can determine how correctly `adudump` functions.

We first tested `adudump` on sequential connections only and then on concurrent connections only. We will consider each of these cases in turn.

5.1 Sequential Validation

These tests produced sequential traffic because the application instances using a TCP connection take turns sending ADUs. That is, they do not send an ADU until they finish receiving the previous ADU. A random packet loss rate of 1% was introduced by FreeBSD's `dummynet` mechanism, which was also used to introduce random per-connection round-trip times. As with application behavior we use plausible randomized network path conditions to test `adudump`, but we do not claim realism.

Figure 2(a) plots the actual and measured per-direction ADU size distributions. The distributions are nearly identical. The slight differences are because, in the case of TCP retransmission timeouts (with sufficiently long RTT), `adudump` splits the ADUs, guessing (incorrectly in this case) that the application intended them to be distinct. The default *quiet time threshold*, which governs this behavior, is 500 milliseconds, so RTTs shorter than this threshold do not split the ADU. We chose 500 ms as a reasonable trade-off between structural detail and solid inference of application intent.

Similarly, Figure 2(b) plots the actual and measured think-time distributions. Note that the actual distributions were different for each direction. Note also

---

[5] `adudump`, which uses CAIDA's CoralReef library, works equally well analyzing offline traces.

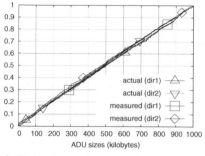

(a) CDF of actual vs. measured ADU size distributions, for either direction.

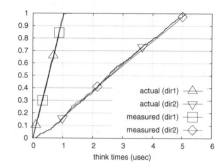

(b) CDF of actual vs. measured think-time distributions, for either direction.

Fig. 2. Sequential validation results

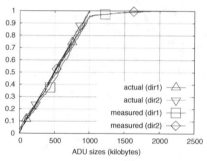

(a) CDF of actual vs. measured ADU size distributions, for either direction.

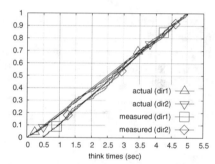

(b) CDF of actual vs. measured think-time distributions, for either direction.

Fig. 3. Concurrent validation results

that, unlike ADU sizes, adudump cannot exactly determine the actual time, because some non-negligible time elapses between the application's timestamp and the monitor's packet capture. Even so, adudump's measurements are very close to the ground truth.

5.2   Concurrent Validation

In the concurrent tests, each application instance sends multiple ADUs with interspersed think times without synchronizing on the ADUs they receive. We did not introduce packet loss in this case.

Figure 3(a) plots the actual and measured per-direction ADU size distributions. The measured data tracks the actual data well for most of the distribution, but diverges in the tail, demonstrating an important limitation of adudump's passive inference abilities: if one of the applications in a concurrent connection has a genuine application-level think time between ADU transmissions that is less than the quiet-time threshold, then adudump will not detect it, and it combines

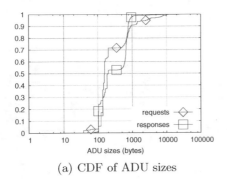
(a) CDF of ADU sizes

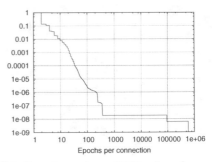
(b) Complementary CDF of exchanges per connection

Fig. 4. Connection structure information inferred by `adudump` for example server

the two ADUs into one that is larger. This is a type of inference error that is unavoidable because we do not have access to applications running on end systems. Nevertheless, this is a sacrifice we gladly make, because it enables generic access to the behavior of any server without any server instrumentation.

Figure 3(b) plots the actual and measured quiet-time distributions. The measured distributions track well with the actual distributions except that, as expected, there are no think times less than 500 ms, the quiet-time threshold.

6   Example Use

The UNC dataset contains records for every server on campus that communicated with a client on the Internet. To demonstrate the usefulness of the data generated by `adudump`, we examine the data pertaining to one such server, the UNC webmail server. We selected this server more-or-less randomly from among many popular UNC servers, yet this example shows the breadth and depth of information available for any servers. Note that the information we present here only scratches the surface of what is available for the webmail server (let alone all UNC servers) and is presented merely to provide an example of the types of analyses that are enabled by `adudump` data.

We start by looking at the broad picture offered by our 6-month dataset. Figure 4(a) shows distributions of request sizes received by the webmail server and response sizes sent by the server. The requests in particular exhibit strong modality, with most of the distribution found in relatively few values. Because we know the identity and purpose of this server, we can conjecture that the smooth increase in response size between 500 and 1,000 bytes is because the size of email messages vary smoothly in that range. We can also make educated guesses about the behavior of these connections, given the (externally known) fact that we are dealing with a HTTPS server. However, without additional information (or system administrator knowledge), we cannot know for certain whether this is the cause. This weakness, however, is also a strength: the bluntness of the

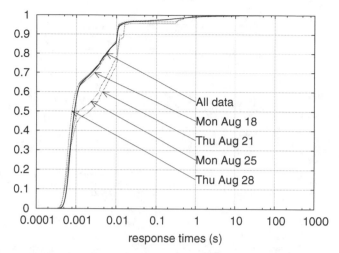

Fig. 5. CDF of response times for example server, both for the entire dataset and during selected days at the start of the semester

inferences that adudump makes also enables it to be more broadly applicable to *any* server operating over TCP.

Another structure-revealing metric is the number of request-response exchanges per connection. Figure 4(b) shows the distribution of exchanges per connection over the entire trace. 86% of connections have exactly two exchanges, 96% have four or fewer, and the distribution exhibits classic heavy-tailed behavior. This plot clearly suggests many avenues for additional analyses (which we are pursuing). Our point in this paper is that adudump provides insight into interesting and important application-level behaviors without requiring any knowledge of what the application is or how it performs.

We also want to briefly explore the depth of data reported by adudump. Figure 5 compares the overall distribution of webmail response times gathered over the whole dataset with specific days. In general, this distribution is very stable from day to day, differing little even on weekends and holidays. However, we discovered a significant change during the beginning of the fall 2008 semester. Monday, August 18th is the day before the start of the semester, and webmail response times for this day are typical. Over the next several days, however, the server takes longer to respond. Normal operation resumes by Thursday the 28th. Although beyond the scope of this paper, we note that it is easy to drill down, looking at response time distributions per hour, differences in request size or response size distributions, or even a timeseries of the individual response time measurements.

7 Case Study

One challenge we face is in detecting when performance anomalies occur, given the quantitative and qualitative variation of response time distributions among

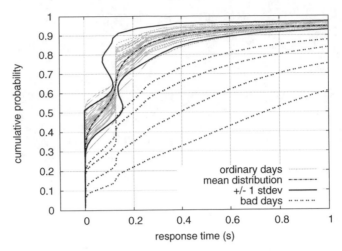

Fig. 6. Illustration of performance anomaly detection using data from a campus web server

servers. First, we note that, for our purposes, it makes little sense to compare response time distributions for different servers. Even servers of the same type (e.g. HTTP) will often have substantially different response time distributions. Thus, we must compare a server's current operation (e.g., the distribution over the past hour or past day) to the same server's historical operation. The problem of performance anomaly detection reduces to determining the likelihood of the current distribution, given the historical distribution (both of which are empirical, or non-parametric).

Figure 6 illustrates this process using two sets of distributions. The lighter lines are CDFs of the response time distribution for a UNC web server for an "ordinary" day. We refer to these as the "training" set. The four dashed lines are response time distributions for days that were flagged by server administrators as corresponding to days when performance problems were noted. In addition, there is a line representing the mean distribution of the training set as well as two lines representing the mean plus or minus one standard deviation.

The standard deviations were calculated using a method introduced in [8]. Each distribution was represented as a 40-bin quantile function. A quantile function can be thought of as a summarized inverse CDF. The distribution is first evenly divided by quantile into 40 bins, so that, for example, the second bin contains all values between the 2.5 and 5th percentiles. Each bin is then summarized as a mean. The result is a vector of length 40, which can be thought of as a point in 40-dimensional space. Principal components analysis (PCA) was then performed on the 40-dimensional "cloud" of points to determine the two (orthogonal) directions of greatest variation, as well as the standard deviation along these axes. Adding and subtracting these principal components (scaled by their respective standard deviations) from the mean gives us an idea of the "spread" of the overall population of distributions. The resulting sum (and difference) give us the 1-standard-deviation "bounds", as shown in Figure 6. The days marked as "bad" fall well outside of the bounds, and thus are clearly anomalous. This provides evidence that anomalous response times can be automatically detected given a historical archive or response time distributions.

8 Conclusion

We have developed and validated a tool to passively infer the application-level dialog in a TCP connection, for all connections on a link, in a passive, online, streaming fashion, at gigabit speeds, on off-the-shelf hardware. Having acquired a multi-month dataset of all TCP connections entering the UNC campus, we have shown that it is possible to identify server response time performance anomalies without knowledge of the function or operation of the server. We believe our tools and methods enable a new paradigm of passive network and server management wherein high-level application performance data can be gleaned from low-level network measurements.

References

1. Feldmann, A.: BLT: Bi-Layer Tracing of HTTP and TCP/IP. In: Proc. of WWW-9 (2000)
2. Olshefski, D.P., Nieh, J., Nahum, E.: ksniffer: determining the remote client perceived response time from live packet streams. In: Proc. OSDI, pp. 333–346 (2004)
3. Olshefski, D., Nieh, J.: Understanding the management of client perceived response time. In: ACM SIGMETRICS Performance Evaluation Review, pp. 240–251 (2006)
4. Smith, F., Hernández-Campos, F., Jeffay, K.: What TCP/IP Protocol Headers Can Tell Us About the Web. In: Proceedings of ACM SIGMETRICS 2001 (2001)
5. Weigle, M.C., Adurthi, P., Hernández-Campos, F., Jeffay, K., Smith, F.: Tmix: a tool for generating realistic TCP application workloads in ns-2. ACM SIGCOMM CCR 36(3), 65–76 (2006)
6. Hernández-Campos, F.: Generation and Validation of Empirically-Derived TCP Application Workloads. Ph.D. dissertation, Dept. of Computer Science, UNC Chapel Hill (2006)
7. Hernández-Campos, F., Jeffay, K., Smith, F.: Modeling and Generation of TCP Application Workloads. In: Proc. IEEE Int'l Conf. on Broadband Communications, Networks, and Systems (September 2007)
8. Broadhurst, R.E.: Compact Appearance in Object Populations Using Quantile Function Based Distribution Families. Ph.D. dissertation, Dept. of Computer Science, UNC Chapel Hill (2008)

GTVS: Boosting the Collection of Application Traffic Ground Truth*

Marco Canini[1,**], Wei Li[2], Andrew W. Moore[2], and Raffaele Bolla[1]

[1] DIST, University of Genoa, Italy
[2] Computer Laboratory, University of Cambridge, UK

Abstract. Interesting research in the areas of traffic classification, network monitoring, and application-oriented analysis can not proceed without real traffic traces, labeled with actual application information. However, hand-labeled traces are an extremely valuable but scarce resource in the traffic monitoring and analysis community, as a result of both privacy concerns and technical difficulties. Hardly any possibility exists for payloaded data to be released, while the impossibility of obtaining certain ground-truth application information from non-payloaded data has severely constrained the value of anonymized public traces.

The usual way to obtain the ground truth is fragile, inefficient and not directly comparable from one's work to another. This paper proposes a methodology and details the design of a technical framework that significantly boosts the efficiency in compiling the application traffic ground truth. Further, a case study on a 30 minute real data trace is presented. In contrast with past work, this is an easy hands-on tool suite dedicated to save user's time and labor and is freely available to the public.

1 Introduction

The collection of ground-truth application information of the Internet traffic is critical to both the research community and the industry:

- it is the basis to build and the only way to evaluate applications for network monitoring, information assurance, and traffic accounting,
- it facilitates the research on nearly every aspect related to applications, protocols, network modelling and data analysis, and
- it provides accurate knowledge of how people use the network which is increasingly important for network security and management.

However, due to privacy concerns, hardly any payloaded data can be released, while publicly accessible non-payloaded traces (e.g., LBNL and MAWI) are of limited value without the associated application information. A common practice becomes to obtain the ground truth from payloaded traces by hand.

---

* This work was supported by the Engineering and Physical Sciences Research Council through grant GR/T10510/02 http://www.cl.cam.ac.uk/research/srg/netos/brasil/

** This work was done while Marco Canini was visiting the Computer Laboratory, University of Cambridge.

Many different, although inherently similar, approaches have been used in the past to obtain the ground truth: Moore and Papagiannaki [1] documented a fine-grained classification scheme comprising nine identification methods. The ground-truth labels used in [2] were based on "hand-classification", while the authors in [3] and [4] were using an "automated payload-based classification" as they described. The collection of many (if not all) of these ground-truth data was automated using extensible NIDSes such as Snort and Bro, or through homemade scripts. The efforts made to collect the ground-truth data were both significant and highly improvised, causing a lot of unnecessary, repeated labor, untrustworthy results (e.g., ground truth derived by signature matching alone) and inconsistency (e.g., different levels of completeness) between different works. Further, there is often a lack of verification mechanisms between multiple information sources, hence faults are inevitable and unrecoverable.

In this paper, we present GTVS (Ground Truth Verification System), a novel framework and methodology dedicated to boost the collection of application ground truth. It reduces the time and labor required in the process by automating the data manipulation and information retrieval processes as well as significantly increasing the efficiency of the hand-verification methodology. It facilitates validations among many information sources to improve the general quality of the ground truth. It works at a finest granularity of a bi-directional flow defined by the IP 5-tuple (IP addresses, transport ports and protocol) but provides aggregated views that allow for better recognition of the host behaviors and it uses heuristic rules based on multiple criteria that accelerate the verification. It is extensible to allow additional information sources and user-defined heuristics, and to achieve different goals. Finally, it provides a neat and handy platform to facilitate the management of hand-verification projects and to allow experiences and data to be shared among the research community.

The following section reviews and validates an important assumption used in our work. Section 3 presents an overview of the GTVS framework. Then, Section 4 presents a detailed case study on a 30 min trace to guide the readers through our ground-truth verification process. Related work is discussed in Section 5 and Section 6 concludes the paper.

2   Assumption and Validation

We observe that flows belonging to the same service or application often share a subset of the IP 5-tuple, notably, the {dst IP, dst port} and {src IP, dst IP} sub-tuples (where dst refers to the server side). This leads to an assumption that underpins our approach: *flows of the same sub-tuples are associated to the same service or application*. With this, the data can be labeled at high-level aggregations. Similar assumptions are implicitly used in BLINC [3] where traffic is classified using graphlets which essentially resolve into sub-tuples.

The consistency between the application label and the two sub-tuples was validated using two day-long traces [1] which had been previously hand-classified and several segments of most recent data. This consistency assumption holds for most cases with few exceptions as separately discussed below.

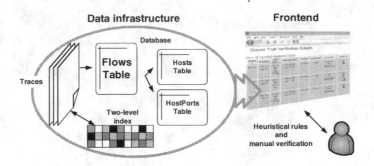

Fig. 1. GTVS: A structure overview

The {dst IP, dst port} sub-tuple. Exceptions are different application encapsulated in VPNs and SOCKS proxies. In our settings, this traffic is currently categorized into the "remote access" class. Others have discussed further mechanisms that can be applied to identify the encapsulated applications [5].

The {src IP, dst IP} sub-tuple. Exceptions include VPNs and SOCKS proxies as well as circumstances where there are multiple applications between a server and a client, e.g., a server operating both an ssh and a web[1] server. However, in such circumstances, the server is usually operating traditional services (e.g., web, ftp, mail or ssh). This sub-tuple effectively complements the one above in classifying applications on multiple ports (e.g., ftp transfers, or P2P).

3   Overview

GTVS can be described as a user-oriented design in a layered structure, as shown in Figure 1. It is composed of **(i)** a basic infrastructure layer for data management including packet traces and flows database, **(ii)** an information-rich frontend from which the user can retrieve all information related to the flows at different aggregations, and **(iii)** a verification process accelerated by flexible heuristic rules. A detailed description for each layer is presented below.

3.1   Data Infrastructure

The data infrastructure processes payloaded traces to collect information on different levels of aggregation (flows, {IP, port} tuples, and hosts).

The trace is organized into files of relatively small size (e.g., 512MB) and is indexed by the timestamp of the first packet contained in each file and by the IP addresses and protocol of each packet therein. The two indexes enable fast queries of the payload content for each flow.

The packets in the trace are aggregated into bi-directional flows and matched against known protocol signatures. For each flow, a number of statistics are

---

[1] In this paper, web-browsing refers to services using a web interface: including web sites and web-based applications such as gmail or youtube.

collected. This information along with the signature-matching results is stored
in the *Flows* table. Based on this table, two further tables are created: namely
the *Hosts* table and *HostPorts* table, to support aggregated views of the traffic
grouped by server or client IPs. These views enable the user to browse the general
behavior on a higher aggregation and also to verify the traffic at this level.

3.2   The Verification Frontend

This second layer consists of a frontend that includes a graphical interface which
presents abundant information at various levels of aggregation, and supports the
use of different kinds of heuristic rules, all to facilitate the verification process.

Combining the merits of many traffic classification works, the information
presented in the frontend is collected from a broad set of sources, including:

- Flow statistics (e.g., duration, number of packets, total number of bytes and
  payload bytes in each direction and TCP flags) as in [2, 6].
- Payload information from a fine-tuned set of protocol signatures as in [1].
- Host name resolution for all the IP addresses appearing in the trace as in [3].[2]
- Port-based mapping using a comprehensive list of well known port numbers.
- Packets payload content (e.g., tcpdump of a flow).
- Host-level connection statistics and transport-layer behavior of the P2P over-
  lay networks as in [7, 3].

Additionally, further information may be available as an extension, such as
data mined from the payload of flows, flow-behavior features as used in [6], or
from external modules (e.g., IDSes, specific traffic analyzers, traffic classifiers).

3.3   Heuristic Rules

The verification frontend also supports the use of heuristic rules. The main idea
is to leverage a core set of automated procedures to verify subsets of similar
flows with very high confidence, while resorting to human discernment when not
enough clues are available to recognize the nature of certain flows.

The heuristics can either be derived empirically or built using a combination
of signature matching results and *a priori* knowledge about known applications,
port numbers and host names. The user can flexibly build his own heuristics,
blending his own site and application-specific knowledge to facilitate desired
tasks. To validate the heuristics, a specific dry-run mode is available for preview-
ing the results of an action before actually modifying the database. On applying
heuristic rules, GTVS will search for potential candidate flows and verify those
which satisfy the conditions given in the heuristics.

In our experience, the use of heuristic rules has allowed us to drastically reduce
the time needed to verify the ground truth.

---

[2] Ideally, the IP addresses should be resolved at the time when the trace is collected.
However, for previously collected traces, host names can be mined from the DNS
traffic in the original trace as well as the Host header field in the HTTP requests,
or, in the worst case, resolved when the trace is being verified.

4   Accelerating the Verification: Experiences with GTVS

The use of GTVS does not replace the manual verification process but is dedicated to accelerating it. Here we suggest two principles, namely those of efficiency and accuracy which we apply to the use of GTVS. The efficiency principle is to always try to work upon higher aggregations (e.g., services rather than individual flows) whenever possible. For example, large numbers of well-known, traditional service traffics on a specific host can be verified in the first instance. The accuracy principle is to make decisions only with very high confidence, e.g., when strong evidence from two or more mutually-independent information sources match with each other.

Normally, the hand verification of an hour-long trace on a 1 Gigabit/s link would take more than a hundred man-hours[3]. With GTVS, we hope an experienced user would be able to verify an initial data trace within days.

In this section, we use the case study for a 30 min trace as an example to introduce the heuristic rules and show how they are exploited to accelerate the verification process. The trace was collected in mid December 2007 from the link to the Internet of a research facility. There were several thousands of users on site, mainly researchers, administrators and technical staff. Table 1 lists the working dimensions of our data set.

Table 1. Working dimensions of our data set

Distinct IPs	Server IPs	Server IP:port pairs	Client IPs	Flows	Packets	Bytes
25,631	11,517	12,198	14,474	250,403	10.9 M	7.4 GB

Because of page limit, we focus on describing how we verified the complete TCP flows, i.e., the flows that are captured entirely from triple handshake to tear down. As for the rest, the UDP flows are verified in a much similar way, except that they are defined using a configurable timeout value. The incomplete TCP flows are typically composed of various kinds of scans and unsuccessful connection attempts. Most of this traffic has distinguishable patterns upon which custom heuristic rules can be built up.

4.1   Initial Application Clues

A set of payload signatures is used in GTVS to help collect the clue of an application from packet payload. Our signature set is capable of identifying 35 most popular protocols. These signatures are derived from databases available on the Web, (e.g., l7-filter[4]). We tested the signatures on previously hand-classified data and several segments of new data. The underspecified signatures which create many false positives (e.g., eDonkey, Skype) have either been changed or

---

[3] An indication from the authors' previous experiences in hand-classification [1].

[4] http://l7-filter.sourceforge.net/

excluded, while the undermatching ones (e.g., BitTorrent) have been improved. Of course, the signatures are still far from being able to identify the totality of the traffic. However, they can be regarded as a useful clue, especially when the results they provide can be co-validated with different evidence.

4.2 The Verification Process (in Iterations)

Our approach is based on a number of successive iterations, each refining the result. Each successive verification iteration focuses upon the remaining unclassified flows about which we have the most confidence. In this way, we can accumulate knowledge based on the highest level of confidence and use this to assist in the classification of data about which we have lower levels of confidence.

Our approach requires the grouping of the heuristics to each iteration and then ordering of the iterations based upon the level of confidence we are able to place in the classification outcome.

We have derived a set of heuristics of which a core subset is presented here. We consider this subset contains those heuristics that provide sufficient generality to be useful for a wide range of applications across different physical sites.

First iteration. Based on the assumption introduced and justified in Section 2, we derive some simple heuristics below.

If the signature matching results for a specific server:port endpoint appear to be strongly consistent, we can reasonably assume that we have identified a particular service on that endpoint. Several criteria are used to quantitatively justify the consistency: thresholds are specified to guarantee that at least a certain percentage of flows as well as a minimum number of flows have matched a specific signature. In addition, only a given subset of signatures is allowed to have matched the flows. For example, it is known that HTTP might appear in BitTorrent[5] traffic, but BitTorrent should not appear in the flows toward a Web server. This constraint is expressed by defining a subset of possible signatures (which does not include BitTorrent when the heuristic is used for HTTP traffic). The thresholds are initially set in a conservative way (e.g., at least 90% and 10 flows), and will be tuned in the third iteration. We apply this heuristic for most of the protocols, especially for those with a well-established signature.

The next heuristics are based on the assumption that flows between the same IP addresses pair are likely due to the same application. For example, FTP traffic between two hosts can be easily verified by considering a host that has an already verified FTP service (e.g., using the first heuristic) and a number of flows each going to a different high port number on the same destination in an incremental fashion. As another example, consider the HTTPS protocol. In many cases a web server is running both standard and secure HTTP services. If a standard HTTP service has been verified on port 80, and a certain fraction of flows to port 443 matches the SSL signature, then the flows between a hosts pair can be heuristically verified. Other similar heuristics can be derived for streaming and

---

[5] BitTorrent clients use HTTP in some of their communications.

Table 2. Traffic breakdown by class and evolution of completeness by iteration

Class	Total			Number of flows by iterations				
	Flows	Packets	Bytes [MB]	1st	2nd	3rd	4th	5th
email	10,871	808,272	470.55	7,225	8,743	9,439	10,420	10,871
ftp	555	894,805	838.22	555	555	555	555	555
gaming	150	2,882	0.47	0	108	108	108	150
im	506	21,036	4.18	65	503	505	505	506
malicious	4,008	62,259	5.30	0	0	0	0	4,008
p2p	17,851	1,125,766	685.43	12,046	12,046	12,728	17,708	17,851
remote	317	135,735	109.26	254	254	254	254	317
services	618	16,675	9.22	466	604	610	610	618
streaming	11	17,815	16.33	0	2	8	8	11
voip	1,043	52,020	11.92	0	121	121	1,042	1,043
web-browsing	212,432	7,630,649	4,889.80	207,888	208,313	211,522	211,522	212,432
unknown	2,041	112,840	52.66	21,904	19,154	14,553	7,671	2,041

VoIP applications: for example, RTSP appear within a TCP control channel while the data are relayed on a unidirectional UDP stream; instead a VoIP application may use a SIP session and a bi-directional UDP stream.

Second iteration. A great amount of information can be derived from the host names. For very popular services (e.g., Google, MSN, eBay), heuristics based on domain names can be easily defined: e.g., HTTPS traffic to MSN servers is due to MSN messenger instead of browsers as well as traffic on port 1863. Further, assuming the trace was captured at the edge of a certain network, specific site information about the internal services and traffic policies can be used to efficiently verify a part of the traffic.

Third iteration. Now we try to lower the thresholds of the previous heuristics. We focus on particular hosts where certain flows are matched by a specific signature, while a part of flows are not matched. If also these flows correspond to the same application, the thresholds can be lowered for those hosts.

Fourth iteration. In this iteration we consider behavioral characteristics of hosts in regard to overlay networks, mainly for the identification of P2P traffic. A typical example, however, is the SMTP traffic which has a strong P2P-like behavior in that SMTP servers act as both the recipient and the sender of emails. The assumption is that if a host is an SMTP server, all the flows generated from this host toward port 25 are mail traffic. In general, this heuristic is applicable for P2P traffic as long as the information about the port number can be utilized[6] and the assumption of the heuristic can be validated. In our experience, for example, there is a large number of eDonkey flows which can be identified using port 4662 and for BitTorrent on port 6881. This heuristic can re-iterate through the data set until no new flows are discovered.

Additionally, for P2P applications that use dynamic port numbers, we resort to a heuristic that considers the host activities and their relationship with a

---

[6] We observe that many P2P nodes still use the well-known port numbers.

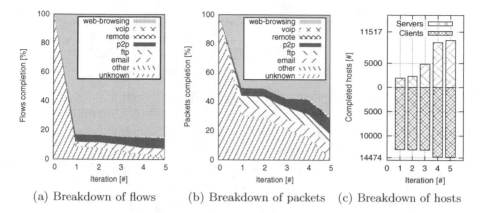

(a) Breakdown of flows   (b) Breakdown of packets   (c) Breakdown of hosts

Fig. 2. Verification completeness against successive iterations

certain overlay network. We select an initial set of peers which are known to run a particular P2P application: some P2P nodes are already identified in the first iteration, and some Skype clients are identified in the second iteration using the information of login servers.[7] Then, for each identified peer, we consider the set of hosts that it communicates with. We select the subset of hosts corresponding to the intersection of all these host sets. Lastly, we identify hosts that are likely peers by applying a threshold (e.g., ≥ 3) on the host's connection degree (i.e., how many peers are connected to this host) and selecting those hosts that do not have other conflicting activities (e.g., if they run multiple P2P applications).

Fifth iteration. From our experience, at this iteration only a small number of payloaded flows remain. User-defined heuristics can be derived according to the specific applications in the analyzed trace, or to the particular behaviors that might be found through manual inspection. Also, based on information of the already verified hosts, one can start to label the incomplete TCP flows and unknown UDP flows, using the assumption on the sub-tuple consistency.

So far, the heuristic rules have greatly reduced the time to verify the flows, although manual verification of a small amount of remaining traffic is still necessary, especially for the identification of new applications.

Table 2 summarizes the total traffic breakdown as we verified, and shows the partial results measured at the end of each iteration, which are graphically presented in Figures 2a and 2b for two metrics: flows and packets. Finally, Figure 2c reports the evolution of completeness for clients and servers during each iteration. As can be seen, a very small number of clients are responsible for the 2,041 unknown flows toward 1,736 servers. In this case, these hosts happen to simultaneously run several P2P applications and we are not able to determine a final conclusion on the specific application.

---

[7] For identifying Skype clients we also use another heuristic based on the peculiarity of this application receiving TCP connection on ports 80 and 443 plus a high number chosen at random.

Table 3. Evaluation of l7-filter's per-class accuracy

Class	False negatives [%]			False positives [%]		
	Flows	Packets	Bytes	Flows	Packets	Bytes
email	25.99	22.33	21.75	0.00	0.00	0.00
ftp	81.26	99.53	99.97	0.00	0.00	0.00
gaming	100.00	100.00	100.00	0.00	0.00	0.00
im	74.90	79.60	81.78	0.00	0.00	0.00
malicious	100.00	100.00	100.00	0.00	0.00	0.00
p2p	16.75	16.65	14.67	0.34	1.85	2.10
remote	18.93	0.52	0.04	0.00	0.00	0.00
services	98.54	99.48	99.94	0.00	0.00	0.00
streaming	27.27	0.15	0.02	0.00	0.00	0.00
voip	100.00	100.00	100.00	0.00	0.00	0.00
web-browsing	0.29	0.42	0.40	0.42	0.52	0.27

Finally, we evaluate l7-filter's accuracy based on the obtained ground truth. Table 3 shows per-class false negatives and positives. Its signatures do not significantly over match, yielding to very few false positives. However, with the exception of web-browsing class, all classes exhibit many false negatives. This is due to two major factors: underspecified signatures and obfuscated traffic. In both cases, our method can exploit information about traffic aggregates to derive the actual application and produce accurate ground truth.

4.3   Discussion

Here we have focused on describing the verification of application traffic. The verification processes of malicious and unwanted traffic (left out due to page limit) are also in progressive development, based on their specific patterns.

One can see that the first-time use of GTVS on any given trace will often require inspection of small segments of data throughout the process, in customizing and testing new heuristics, dry-runs, tuning thresholds, and final manual decisions on hard objects. However, if one is carrying out a continuous ground truth collection work on a specific site or on many sites simultaneously, time would be further saved as we expect only limited tuning and validation are needed.

Since this framework will become publicly available, it is also easier to share the knowledge within the community: not only the string signatures but also the heuristics and application-specific knowledge would become a public resource and can be constructed and validated by any user of this framework.

We also note that the confidence of the ground truth verified by GTVS relies mainly on its user. Therefore to collect good ground truth requires sufficient user interactions and dry-runs to double-confirm the user's judgments.

5   Related Work

On the technical aspects, our work can be seen as a cumulative progress, with lots of inspirations from previous traffic classification works, including [2,3,6,7,8,9].

Each of these works made use of a different set of information sources, which are combined in our framework.

A content-based classification scheme comprising of nine identification methods was presented in [1]. Despite their highly accurate and complete results, there was not a systematic infrastructure or an indication of how the procedure can be organized. Thus a barrier exists preventing other people from repeating their method. Further, GTVS uses a broader set of information sources.

In [10], the authors suggested a technique based on active measurements to cover the shortage of ground-truth data. This work is tackling a similar problem to ours. However, we argue that this technique is incapable of delivering the variety and fidelity of real traffic. In contrast, we focus on maximally reducing the time and labor necessary to obtain accurate ground truth from real traffic.

6 Conclusions

In this paper, we presented the novel Ground Truth Verification System (GTVS). A detailed guide is shown on how to use GTVS to accelerate the verification process, as well as the results by iterations from a case study of real traffic. Further, we are publicly releasing this system and our rule sets. It is hoped that it will substantially save the time and labor for individual researchers, and more public data with ground-truth labels may subsequently become available to the community in the near future.

References

1. Moore, A.W., Papagiannaki, D.: Toward the accurate identification of network applications. In: Dovrolis, C. (ed.) PAM 2005. LNCS, vol. 3431, pp. 41–54. Springer, Heidelberg (2005)
2. Moore, A.W., Zuev, D.: Internet traffic classification using bayesian analysis techniques. In: Proceedings of ACM SIGMETRICS 2005, pp. 50–60 (2005)
3. Karagiannis, T., Papagiannaki, K., Faloutsos, M.: Blinc: multilevel traffic classification in the dark. In: Proceedings of ACM SIGCOMM 2005, pp. 229–240 (2005)
4. Erman, J., et al.: Traffic classification using clustering algorithms. In: Proceedings of the SIGCOMM workshop on mining network data, MineNet 2006 (2006)
5. Dusi, M., et al.: Tunnel hunter: Detecting application-layer tunnels with statistical fingerprinting. Computer Networks 53(1), 81–97 (2009)
6. Li, W., Moore, A.W.: A machine learning approach for efficient traffic classification. In: Proceedings of IEEE MASCOTS 2007 (October 2007)
7. Karagiannis, T., Broido, A., Faloutsos, M., Claffy, K.: Transport layer identification of P2P traffic. In: Proceedings of Internet Measurement Conference (2004)
8. Trestian, I., Ranjan, S., Kuzmanovic, A., Nucci, A.: Unconstrained endpoint profiling (googling the internet). In: Proceedings of ACM SIGCOMM 2008, pp. 279–290 (2008)
9. Dreger, H., et al.: Dynamic application-layer protocol analysis for network intrusion detection. In: 15th USENIX Security Symposium (2006)
10. Szabó, G., et al.: On the validation of traffic classification algorithms. In: Claypool, M., Uhlig, S. (eds.) PAM 2008. LNCS, vol. 4979, pp. 72–81. Springer, Heidelberg (2008)

TIE: A Community-Oriented Traffic Classification Platform

Alberto Dainotti, Walter de Donato, and Antonio Pescapé

University of Napoli "Federico II", Italy
{alberto,walter.dedonato,pescape}@unina.it

Abstract. The research on network traffic classification has recently become very active. The research community, moved by increasing difficulties in the automated identification of network traffic, started to investigate classification approaches alternative to port-based and payload-based techniques. Despite the large quantity of works published in the past few years on this topic, very few implementations targeting alternative approaches have been made available to the community. Moreover, most approaches proposed in literature suffer of problems related to the ability of evaluating and comparing them. In this paper we present a novel community-oriented software for traffic classification called TIE, which aims at becoming a common tool for the fair evaluation and comparison of different techniques and at fostering the sharing of common implementations and data. Moreover, TIE supports the combination of more classification plugins in order to build multi-classifier systems, and its architecture is designed to allow online traffic classification.

1 Introduction

The problem of traffic classification (i.e. associating traffic flows to the applications that generated them) has attracted increasing research efforts in recent years. This happened because, lately, the traditional approach of relying on transport-level protocol ports has become largely unreliable [1], pushing the search for alternative techniques. At first, research and industry focused on approaches based on payload inspection. However, such techniques present several drawbacks in realistic scenarios, e.g.: (i) their large computational cost makes difficult to use them on high-bandwidth links; (ii) requiring full access to packet payload poses concerns related to user privacy; (iii) they are typically unable to cope with traffic encryption and protocol obfuscation techniques. For these reasons, the research community started proposing classification approaches that consider other properties of traffic, typically adopting statistical and machine-learning approaches [2] [3] [4]. Despite the large quantity of works published in the past few years on traffic classification, aside from port-based classifiers ([5]) and those based on payload inspection ([6] [7] [8]), there are few implementations made available to the community that target alternative approaches. NetAI [9] is a tool able to extract a set of features both from live traffic and traffic traces.

M. Papadopouli, P. Owezarski, and A. Pras (Eds.): TMA 2009, LNCS 5537, pp. 64–74, 2009.
© Springer-Verlag Berlin Heidelberg 2009

However it does not directly perform traffic classification, but relies on external tools to use the extracted features for such purpose. To the best of our knowledge the only available traffic classifier implementing a machine-learning technique presented in literature is Tstat 2.0 [10] (released at the end of October 2008). Besides supporting classification through payload inspection, Tstat 2.0 is able to identify Skype traffic by using the techniques described in [11]. However such techniques have been specifically designed for a single application and can not be extended to classify overall link traffic. The lack of available implementations of novel approaches is in contrast with two facts: (i) scientific papers seem to confirm that it is possible to classify traffic by using properties different from payload content; (ii) there are strong motivations for traffic classification in general, and important reasons to perform it without relying on packet content. It has been observed that the novel approaches proposed in literature suffer of problems related to the ability of evaluating and comparing them [12]. A first reason for this difficulty is indeed the lack of implementations allowing third parties to test the techniques proposed with different traffic traces and under different situations. However, there are also difficulties related to, e.g., differences in the objects to be classified (flows, TCP connections, etc.), or in the considered classes (specific applications, application categories, etc.), as well as regarding the metrics used to evaluate classification performance.

To overcome these limitations, in this work we introduce a novel software tool for traffic classification called *Traffic Identification Engine* (TIE). TIE has been designed as a community-oriented tool, inspired by the above observations, to provide researchers and practitioners a platform to easily develop (and make available) implementations of traffic classification techniques and to allow fair comparisons among them. In the following sections, when presenting TIE's components and functionalities, we detail some of the design choices focused on: multi-classification, comparison of approaches, and online traffic classification.

2 Operating Modes

Before describing the architecture and the functionalities we introduce the three operating modes of TIE. Their operation will be further detailed in the next sections.

- **Offline Mode:** information regarding the classification of a session is generated only when the session ends or at the end of TIE execution. This operating mode is typically used by researchers evaluating classification techniques, when there are no timing constraints regarding classification output and the user needs information related to the entire session lifetime.
- **Realtime Mode:** information regarding the classification of a session is generated as soon as it is available. This operating mode implements *online* classification. The typical application is policy enforcement of classified traffic (QoS, Admission Control, Billing, Firewalling, etc.). Strict timing and memory constraints are assumed.

- **Cyclic Mode:** information regarding the classification is generated at regular intervals (e.g. each 5 minutes) and stored into separate output files. Each output file contains only data from the sessions that generated traffic during the corresponding interval. An example usage is to build live traffic reporting graphs and web pages.

All working modes can be applied to both live traffic and traffic traces. Obviously, *realtime* mode is the one imposing most constraints to the design of TIE's components. We highlight that TIE was designed since the beginning targeting online classification, and this affected several aspects, described through the next section, of its architecture.

3   Architecture Overview and Functionalities

TIE is written in C language and runs on Unix operating systems, currently supporting Linux and FreeBSD platforms. The software is made of a single executable and a set of plugins dynamically loaded at run time. A collection of utilities is distributed with the sources and are part of the TIE framework. TIE is made of several components, each of them responsible for a specific task. Figure 1 shows the main blocks composing TIE.

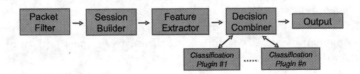

Fig. 1. TIE: main components involved in classification

3.1   Packet Collection and Filtering

As regards packet capture, TIE is based on the Libpcap library [13], which is an open source C library offering an interface for capturing link-layer frames over a wide range of system architectures. Moreover, Libpcap allows to read packets from files in *tcpdump* format (a *de facto* standard [13]) rather than from network interfaces, without modifications to the application's code. This allows to easily write a single application able to work both in realtime and offline conditions.

By supporting the BPF syntax [14], Libpcap allows programmers to write applications that transparently support a rich set of constructs to build detailed packet filtering expressions for most network protocols. Besides supporting the powerful BPF filters, which are called inside the capture driver, we implemented in TIE additional filtering functionalities working in user-space. Examples are: skipping the first m packets, selecting traffic within a specified time range, and checking for headers integrity (TCP checksum, valid fields etc.).

3.2   Sessions

TIE decomposes network traffic into sessions, which are the objects to be classified. In literature approaches that classify different kinds of traffic objects have been presented: flows, TCP connections, hosts, etc. To make TIE support multiple approaches and techniques, we have defined the general concept of session, and specified different definitions of it (selected using command line switches):

- **flow:** Defined by the tuple $\{SRC_{IP}, SRC_{port}, DEST_{IP}, DEST_{port}, transport\text{-}level\ protocol\}$ and an inactivity timeout, with a default value of 60 seconds.
- **biflow:** Defined by the tuple $\{SRC_{IP}, SRC_{port}, DEST_{IP}, DEST_{port}, transport\text{-}level\ protocol\}$, where source and destination can be swapped, and the inactivity timeout is referred to packets in any direction.
- **host:** A host session contains all packets it generates or receives. A timeout can be optionally set.

When the transport protocol is TCP, biflows typically approximate TCP connections. However no checks on connection handshake or termination are made, nor packet retransmissions are considered. This very simple heuristic has been adopted on purpose, because it is computationally light and therefore appropriate for online classification. This definition simply requires a lookup on a hash table for each packet. However, some approaches may require stricter rules to recognize TCP connections, able to identify the start and end of the connections with more accuracy (e.g. relying on features extracted from the first few packets ,as TCP options, or packet sizes [15] [16]). Moreover, explicitly detecting the expiration of a TCP connection avoids its segmentation in several biflows when there are long periods of silence (e.g. Telnet, SSH). For these reasons, we implemented heuristics to follow the state of TCP connections by looking at TCP flags that can be optionally activated:

- If the first packet of a TCP biflow does not contain a SYN flag then it is skipped. This is especially useful to filter out connections initiated before traffic capture was started.
- The creation of a new biflow is forced if a TCP packet containing only a SYN flag is received (i.e. if a TCP biflow with the same tuple was active then it is forced to expire and a new biflow is started).
- A biflow is forced to expire if a FIN flag has been detected in both directions.
- The inactivity timeout is disabled on TCP biflows (they expire only if FIN flags are detected).

These heuristics have been chosen in order to trade-off between computational complexity and accuracy. Some applications, however, may require a more faithful reconstruction of TCP connections. For example payload inspection techniques used for security purposes, may require the correct reassembly of TCP streams in order to not be vulnerable to evasion techniques [17]. For these tasks, a user-space TCP state machine may be integrated into TIE, however this would significantly increase computational complexity.

Some session types (i.e. *biflow* and *host*) contain traffic flowing in two opposite directions, which we call *upstream* and *downstream*. These are defined by looking at the direction of the first packet (upstream direction). Information regarding the two directions must be kept separate, for example to allow extraction of features (e.g. IPT, packet count, etc.) related to a single direction. Therefore, within each session with bidirectional traffic, counters and state information are kept for each direction. In order to keep track of sessions status according to the above definitions we use a chained hash table data structure, in which information regarding each session can be dynamically stored. Each session type is identified by a key of a fixed number of bits. For example, both keys of the *flow* and *biflow* session types contain two IP addresses, two port numbers, and the protocol type.

For each session it is necessary to keep track of some information and to update them whenever a new packet belonging to the same session is processed (e.g. status, counters, features). Also, it is necessary to archive an expired session and to allocate a new structure for a new session. We therefore associate to each item stored in the hash table a linked list of sessions structures. That is, each element of the hash table, which represents a session key, contains a pointer to a linked list of session structures, with the head associated to the currently active session. In order to properly work with high volumes of traffic, TIE is also equipped with a Garbage Collector component that is responsible of keeping clean the session table. At regular intervals it scans the table looking for expired sessions. If necessary it dumps expired sessions data (including classification results) to the output files and it then frees the memory associated to those sessions.

3.3   Feature Extraction

In order to classify sessions, TIE has to collect the features needed by the specific classification plugins activated. The Feature Extractor is the component in charge of collecting classification features and it is triggered by the Session Builder for every incoming packet. To avoid unnecessary computations and memory occupation, most features can be collected on-demand by specifying command line options. This is particularly relevant when we want to perform online classification. The calculation of features is indeed a critical element affecting the computational load of a classifier. In [15] the computational complexity and memory overhead of some features in the context of online classification are indeed evaluated. We started implementing basic features used by most classifiers, considering techniques of different categories: port-based, flow-based, payload inspection. We plan to enlarge the list of supported features by considering both new kinds of features and sets published in literature [18]. Classification features extracted from each session are kept in the same session structure stored in the hash table previously described. In general, each session structure contains: (i) basic information (e.g. the session key, a session identifier, partial or final classification results, status flags, etc.); (ii) timing information (e.g. timestamps of the last seen packet for each direction); (iii) counters (e.g. number of bytes and packets for each direction, number of packets without payload, etc.); (iv) optional classification features (e.g. payload size and inter-packet time vectors, a payload stream from the first few packets, etc.).

3.4 Classification

TIE provides a multi-decisional engine made of a Decision Combiner (*DC* in the following) and one or more Classification Plugins (or shortly classifiers) implementing different classification techniques. Each classifier is a standalone dynamically loadable software module. At runtime, a *Plugin Manager* is responsible of searching and loading classification plugins according to a configuration file called *enabled_plugins*.

```
typedef struct classifier {
    int (*disable) ();
    int (*enable) ();
    int (*load_signatures) (char *);
    int (*train) (char *);
    class_output *(*classify_session) (void *session);
    int (*dump_statistics) (FILE *);
    bool (*is_session_classifiable) (void *session);
    int (*session_sign) (void *session, void *packet);

    char *name;
    char *version;
    u_int32_t *flags;
} classifier;
```

Fig. 2. TIE: interface of classification plugins

Classification plugins have a standard interface, shown in Figure 2. To help plugin developers, a *dummy* plugin with detailed internal documentation is distributed with TIE. Moreover the other classification plugins distributed with TIE can serve as sample reference code. After loading a plugin, the Plugin Manager calls the corresponding *enable*() function, which is in charge of verifying if all the features needed are available (some features are enabled by command line options). If some features are missing, then the plugin is disabled by calling the *disable*() function. After enabling a plugin, the *load_signatures*() function is called in order to load classification fingerprints. The *DC* is responsible for the classification of sessions and it implements the strategy used for the combination of multiple classifiers. Whenever a new packet associated to an unclassified session arrives, after updating session status information and extracting features, TIE calls the *DC*. For each session, the *DC* must make four choices: if a classification attempt is to be made, when (and if) each classifier must be invoked (possibly multiple times), when the final classification decision is taken, how to combine the classification outputs from the classification plugins into the final decision. To take these decisions and to coordinate the activity of multiple classifiers, the *DC* operates on a set of session flags and invokes, for each classification plugin, two functions in the *classifier* structure: *is_session_classifiable()* and *classify_session()*. The *is_session_classifiable*() function asks a classifier

```
typedef struct class_output {
    u_int16_t id;          /* Application id */
    u_int8_t subid;        /* Application sub id */
    u_int8_t confidence;   /* Confidence value */
    u_int32_t flags;
} class_output;
```

Fig. 3. The class_output structure stores the output of a classification attempt

if enough information is available for it to attempt a classification of the current session. The *classify_session*() function performs the actual classification attempt, returning the result in a *class_output* structure, shown in Figure 3.

To highlight the central role of the *DC* and how it is possible, with few functions and structures, to design flexible decision strategies, in the following we illustrate some sample situations regarding the four main decision mentioned above.

- **When to attempt classification.** The *DC* could decide to not evaluate the current session depending on information from the classification plugins or on a priori basis. The latter may happen, for example, when the target of classification is a restricted set of traffic categories. In the first case, instead, the *DC* typically asks each of the active classification plugins if it is able to attempt classification on the current session. Depending on the replies from the classifiers the *DC* can decide to make a classification attempt.
- **When each classifier must be invoked.** Depending on the classifiers that are available, the *DC* could decide to invoke only some of them, and only at some time, for a certain session. For example, there could be classification techniques that are applicable only to TCP biflows or some classifiers may be invoked only when certain information is present. This is the case of payload-based classifiers. In general, we can design combination strategies with more complicate algorithms, in which the invocation of a specific classifier depends on several conditions and on the output of other classifiers. For example, if a session is recognized as carrying encrypted traffic by a classification plugin, then the *DC* may start a classifier specifically designed for encrypted traffic.
- **When the final classification decision is taken.** The *DC* must decide when TIE has to assign a class to a session. Simple strategies are, e.g., when at least one classifier has returned a result, or when all of them have returned a classification result, etc. In more complicate approaches, this choice can vary depending on the features of the session (e.g. TCP, UDP, number of packets, etc.) and the output of the classifiers. Moreover, if working in *online* mode, a limit on the time elapsed or the number of packets seen since the start of the session is typically set.
- **How to combine the classification outputs from the classification plugins into the final decision.** The *DC* receives a *class_output* structure (Figure 3) from each of the classification plugins invoked. These must then be *fused* into a single final decision. The *class_output* structure contains also a confidence value returned by each of the classifiers, which can be helpful when combining conflicting results from different classifiers, and it determines the

final confidence value returned by the *DC*. Effectively combining conflicting results from different classifiers is a crucial task. The problem of combining classifiers actually represents a research area in the machine-learning field *per se*. Simple static approaches are based on majority and/or priority criteria, whereas more complex strategies can be adopted to take into account the nature of the classifiers and their per-class metrics like accuracy [19].

We distribute TIE with a basic combination strategy as a first sample implementation. For each session, the decision is taken only if all the classifiers that are enabled are ready to classify it. To take its decision the combiner assigns priorities to classifiers according to the order of their appearance in the *enabled_plugins* file. If all the plugins agree on the result, or some of them classify the session as *Unknown*, the combination is straightforward and the final confidence value is computed as the sum of each confidence value divided by the number of enabled plugins. Instead, if one or more plugins disagree, the class is decided by the plugin with highest priority. To take into account the conflicting results of the classifiers, the confidence value is evaluated as before, and then divided by 2. All the code implementing the decision combiner is in separate source files that can be easily modified and extended to write a new combination strategy. After future addition of further classification plugins, we plan to add combination strategies that are more sophisticated.

Finally, it is possible to run TIE with the purpose to train one or more classification plugins implementing machine-learning techniques with data extracted from a traffic trace. To do this, we first need pre-classified data (ground truth). These can be obtained by running TIE on the same traffic trace using a ground-truth classification plugin. The same output file generated by TIE is then used as pre-classified data and given as input to TIE configured to perform a training phase.

3.5   Data Definitions and Output Format

One of the design goals of TIE, was to allow comparison of multiple approaches. For this purpose a unified representation of classification output is needed. More precisely we defined IDs for application classes (*applications*) and propose such IDs as reference. Moreover, several approaches presented in literature classify sessions into classes that are groups of applications offering similar services. We therefore added definitions of *group* classes and assigned each application to a group. This allows to compare a classification technique that classifies traffic into application classes with another classifying traffic into group classes. Moreover, it allows to perform a higher-level comparison between two classifiers that both use application classes, by looking at differences only in terms of groups. To build an application database inside TIE, we started by analyzing those used by the CoralReef suite [5], and by the L7-filter project [7], because they represent the most complete sets that are publicly available and because such tools represent the state of the art in the field of traffic analysis and classification tools. By comparing such two application databases, we then decided to create

```
#AppID SubID GroupID Label        SubLabel          Description
0,     0,    0,      "UNKNOWN",   "UNKNOWN",        "Unknown application"
#
1,     0,    1,      "HTTP",      "HTTP",           "World Wide Web"
1,     1,    1,      "HTTP",      "DAP",            "Download Accelerator Plus"
1,     2,    1,      "HTTP",      "FRESHDOWNLOAD",  "Fresh Download"
1,     7,    1,      "HTTP",      "QUICKTIME",      "Quicktime HTTP"
[...]
10,    0,    3,      "FTP",       "FTP",            "File Transfer Protocol"
10,    1,    3,      "FTP",       "FTP_DATA",       "FTP data stream"
10,    2,    3,      "FTP",       "FTP_CONTROL",    "FTP control"
[...]
4,     0,    1,      "HTTPS",     "HTTPS",          "Secure Web"
5,     0,    9,      "DNS",       "DNS",            "Domain Name Service"
```

Fig. 4. TIE: definitions of application classes from the file *tie_apps.txt*

a more complete one by including information from both sources and trying to preserve most of the definitions in there. To each application class, TIE associates the following information: (i) an identifier, (ii) a human readable label, (iii) a group identifier. To properly define the application groups we started from the categories proposed by [20] and then we extended them by looking at those proposed by CoralReef [5] and L7-filter [7]. Moreover, to introduce a further level of granularity, for each application class we allow the definition of sub-application identifiers in order to discriminate among sessions of the same application generating traffic with different properties (e.g. signaling vs. data, or Skype voice vs. Skype chat, etc.). Figure 4 shows portions of the *tie_apps.txt* file. Each line defines one application identified by the pair $(AppID, SubID)$. The main output file generated by TIE contains information about the sessions processed and their classification. The output file is composed by a header and a body. The header contains details about the whole traffic results, the plugins activated, and the options chosen. The body is a column-separated table whose fields contain the following session related information: a unique identifier, the 5-tuple, the start/end timestamps, the packets/bytes count for both upstream and downstream directions, a $(AppID, SubID)$ pair and a confidence value as resulting from classification process. The output format is unique but counters and timestamps semantics depend on (i) the operating mode and (ii) the session type. In *offline* mode those fields refer to the entire session. In *realtime* mode they refer only to the period between the start of the session and the time at which the classification of the session has been made. This is done to reduce computations to the minimum after a session has been classified. Finally, in *cyclic* mode an output file with a different name is generated for each time interval, and the above-mentioned fields refer only to the current interval.

4   Conclusion

In this paper we introduced a community-oriented software tool for traffic classification called TIE, supporting the fair evaluation and comparison of different techniques and fostering the sharing of common implementations and data. Moreover, TIE is thought as a multi-classifier system and to perform online traffic classification. TIE will allow the experimental study of a number of hot topics in traffic classification, such as:

- *multi-classification*: We are working on the combination of multiple classification techniques with pluggable fusion strategies.
- *sharable data*: We are implementing algorithms to produce pre-labeled and anonymized traffic traces, which will allow the sharing of reference data for comparison and evaluation purposes.
- *privacy*: We are working on the design of lightweight approaches to payload inspection that are privacy-friendly and more suitable for online classification.
- *ground truth*: We are working on developing more accurate approaches for the creation of ground-truth reference data through the combination of multiple and novel techniques.
- *performance analysis*: Disposing of multiple implementations of classification techniques on the same platform allows to fairly compare different techniques *on the field*. TIE will support the measurement of operating variable such as classification time, computational load, as well as memory footprint.

Acknowledgements

This work has been partially supported by he CONTENT EU Network of Excellence (IST-FP6-038423) and by the European Community's Seventh Framework Programme under Grant Agreement No. 216585 (INTERSECTION Project).

References

1. Karagiannis, T., Broido, A., Brownlee, N., Claffy, K.C., Faloutsos, M.: Is p2p dying or just hiding? In: IEEE Globecom (2004)
2. Karagiannis, T., Papagiannaki, K., Faloutsos, M.: Blinc: Multilevel traffic classification in the dark. In: ACM SIGCOMM (August 2005)
3. Auld, T., Moore, A.W., Gull, S.F.: Bayesian neural networks for internet traffic classification. IEEE Transactions on Neural Networks 18(1), 223–239 (2007)
4. Williams, N., Zander, S., Armitage, G.: A preliminary performance comparison of five machine learning algorithms for practical ip traffic flow classification. ACM SIGCOMM CCR 36(5), 7–15 (2006)
5. CoralReef, http://www.caida.org/tools/measurement/coralreef/
6. Paxson, V.: Bro: A system for detecting network intruders in real-time. In: Computer Networks, pp. 23–24 (1999)
7. L7-filter, Application Layer Packet Classifier for Linux, http://l7-filter.sourceforge.net
8. Cisco Systems. Blocking Peer-to-Peer File Sharing Programs with the PIX Firewall, http://www.cisco.com/application/pdf/paws/42700/block_p2p_pix.pdf
9. netAI: Network Traffic based Application Identification, http://caia.swin.edu.au/urp/dstc/netai
10. Tstat (November 2008), http://tstat.tlc.polito.it
11. Bonfiglio, D., Mellia, M., Meo, M., Rossi, D., Tofanelli, P.: Revealing skype traffic: when randomness plays with you. In: SIGCOMM 2007, pp. 37–48. ACM, New York (2007)
12. Salgarelli, L., Gringoli, F., Karagiannis, T.: Comparing traffic classifiers. SIGCOMM Comput. Commun. Rev. 37(3), 65–68 (2007)

13. Tcpdump and the Libpcap library (November 2008), http://www.tcpdump.org
14. Jacobson, V., McCanne, S.: The bsd packet filter: A new architecture for userlevel packet capture. In: Winter 1993 USENIX Conference, January 1993, pp. 259–269 (1993)
15. Li, W., Moore, A.W.: A machine learning approach for efficient traffic classification. In: IEEE MASCOTS (October 2007)
16. Bernaille, L., Teixeira, R., Salamatian, K.: Early application identification. In: ACM CoNEXT (December 2006)
17. Ptacek, T.H., Newsham, T.N.: Insertion, evasion, and denial of service: Eluding network intrusion detection. Technical report (1998)
18. Moore, A., Zuev, D., Crogan, M.: Discriminators for use in flow-based classification. Technical Report RR-05-13, Dept. of Computer Science, Queen Mary, University of London (2005)
19. Kuncheva, L.I.: Combining Pattern Classifiers: Methods and Algorithms. Wiley, Chichester (2004)
20. Moore, A., Papagiannaki, K.: Toward the accurate identification of network applications. In: Dovrolis, C. (ed.) PAM 2005. LNCS, vol. 3431, pp. 41–54. Springer, Heidelberg (2005)

Revealing the Unknown ADSL Traffic Using Statistical Methods

Marcin Pietrzyk[1], Guillaume Urvoy-Keller[2], and Jean-Laurent Costeux[1]

[1] Orange Labs, France
{marcin.pietrzyk,jeanlaurent.costeux}@orange-ftgroup.com
[2] Institute Eurecom, France
{urvoy}@eurecom.fr

Abstract. Traffic classification is one of the most significant issues for ISPs and network administrators. Recent research on the subject resulted in a large variety of algorithms and methods applicable to the problem. In this work, we focus on several issues that have not received enough attention so far. First, the establishment of an accurate reference point. We use an ISP internal Deep Packet Inspection (DPI) tool and confront its results with state of the art, freely available classification tools, finding significant differences. We relate those differences to the weakness of some signatures and to the heuristics and design choices made by DPI tools. Second, we highlight methodological issues behind the choices of the traffic classes and the way of analyzing the results of a statistical classifier. Last, we focus on the often overlooked problem of mining the unknown traffic, i.e., traffic not classified by the DPI tool used to establish the reference point. We present a method, relying on the level of confidence of the statistical classification, to reveal the unknown traffic. We further discuss the result of the classifier using a variety of heuristics.

1 Introduction

Knowledge about the applications that generated a traffic mixture in the network is essential for ISPs and network administrators. It can be used as the input for a number of network planning, charging and performance studies. The objective of traffic classification is to automatically and accurately find out what classes or precise applications are run by the end users. This task, recently becomes more and more challenging. The reason for this lies in the TCP/IP protocol stack design, which is not providing explicit information about the application that generated traffic. Performance of classically used methods, e.g., port based classification, is diminishing due to the development of new applications, which purposely try to evade traffic detection. We observe this behavior on our platform, where half of the traffic on the ftp legacy ports is generated by peer-to-peer applications. The research community reacted with a number of works proposing solutions or possible lines of further inquiry to solve this important problem [1], [3], [5], [7].

In this paper, we put the emphasis on a number of key issues that need to be addressed while performing statistical classification of traffic. A first key issue is the calibration of the statistical classifier. This task is in general addressed using some DPI tool. Considering an hour long TCP trace from a large ADSL platform, we highlight in Section 3

M. Papadopouli, P. Owezarski, and A. Pras (Eds.): TMA 2009, LNCS 5537, pp. 75–83, 2009.

the possible weaknesses of DPI tools and the difficulty of reconciling the results from different tools. Another issue when using any statistical classifier is the choice of the traffic classes, i.e., the desired level of granularity that one wants to achieve, as well as the interpretation of the results of the classifiers. We illustrate those points in Section 5. Last but not least, we focus on the problem of mining the unknown traffic, i.e., the traffic that the DPI tool failed to identify. This is indeed the ultimate goal of a classifier to be applied in the wild and it is important to see what it can extract when DPI techniques fail. We discuss in Section 6 how a classifier can be used for this task and propose several heuristics to confirm the results.

2   Areas of Improvement

In this section, we describe in more details several issues that are often overlooked while experimenting with statistical classification tools. We further illustrate them in Sections 3 to 6 using a trace captured on a large ADSL platform.

Reference point. As already mentioned, in order to assess the accuracy of any method used, a good reference point[1] is required. This point often does not get enough attention. There are many reasons behind this fact. First, it is in general difficult to obtain relevant traces containing application payload. Second, the design of application signatures is a complex task. Let us consider the case of the eMule application. A signature commonly used [3,7] test for the presence of the /(xe3 or xc5)/ bytes in the payload. It has two drawbacks. First, it can lead to a high fraction of false positives. Second, since 2006, eMule is supporting protocol obfuscation, which makes this simple signature missing an important fraction of eMule flows. DPI tools not only rely on signatures but also feature some heuristics to flag application traffic. As an example, authors in [3] deal with the eMule encryption issue by assuming that all unclassified flows of the end users who have at least one flow classified as eMule are due to eMule. This approach might sometimes be misleading, for instance in the simple case where the user runs eMule in parallel with another encrypted service. We further investigate the problem of reference point establishment by comparing 3 DPI tools in Section 3.

Traffic classes definition. Traffic classes can be defined in different ways. Some papers provide a very coarse grained division; others focus on the detection of a single protocol. It makes comparisons difficult. We approach this problem by performing a two level study. First, we apply our methods against a coarse-grained classes definition. Second, we divide the peer-to-peer class into four subclasses, each containing a single application. We discuss the accuracy of the method in the two cases in Section 5.

Unknown class. Most of the studies follow the same schema. They calibrate one or several statistical methods using a fraction of pre-labeled flows and test its accuracy over larger, classified sets. However, no matter how good the DPI tool is, there remains a fraction of traffic not classified. This traffic class, which accounts for as large as 60% of the flows in some cases (e.g., [7]) is put aside. In the best case, the authors obtain

---

[1] What we term reference point in this work is often called 'ground truth' in the literature.

classifiers that are as good as the refference point provided by the DPI tool. In practice, the classification of the unknown traffic is a key issue. We address this problem in two ways in Section 6. First, we use our (best) classifier over the unknown class of traffic and report on its predictions assuming specific confidence levels. Next, we investigate several heuristics, based on endpoints profiling to back up the statistical tool output.

3   Reference Point Issue

We used three DPI tools and compare their results on an example ADSL trace which high level description is provided in in Section 4:

- A tool based on Bro [9] that implements the set of signatures used by Erman in [3], as extracted from the technical report of the same author;
- An internal tool called Claude that is constantly developed and tested at Orange;
- Tstat v2 [11] that features DPI functions.

The results with Bro turned out to be deceiving, with more than 55% of unknown flows. A more detailed inspection of over thirty of the signatures used, revealed that most of them are outdated.

We thus decided to focus our comparison on Claude and Tstat only. Claude is used for network analysis and dimensioning. It is capable of detecting several terms of applications, including encrypted ones. It combines several methods of traffic classification, from deep packet inspection to methods as sophisticated as parsing the signaling messages of an application in order to extract endpoint IPs and ports. Claude is constantly developed and tested on several sites in France.

To compare Tstat to Claude we need to devise a set of application classes that both tools detect. We consider the following set: Web, eDonkey, BitTorrent, Ares and Mail. We will use more classes in Section 4.

Results of the comparison between Tstat and Claude are depicted in Table 1. We report the breakdown of flows obtained using each tool and also the overlap between the two tools taking the union of both sets as a reference for each class. For p2p applications, the agreement is very good, in each case higher than 90%. For Mail and Web, we have more significant differences. A closer look at Web traffic revealed that the difference between the two tools is mostly due to Claude identifying more Web transfers than Tstat. This additional set of flows consists of a large fraction of connections to port 443 - https service - or flows with less than three packets. This most probably explains why Tstat did not classify them as Web. As for the Web flows identified by Tstat only, they appeared to be mostly due to streaming applications over http, e.g., YouTube video streaming. Tstat labels those flows as Web while Claude labels them as Http Streaming. While there is a limited number of such flows, they carry a significant amount of bytes, which leads to a more pronounced disagreement between Tstat and Claude when focusing on bytes rather than flows. More generally, looking at bytes provides a different picture. For instance, for the case of eDonkey, Tstat and Claude agree for only 50% of the bytes. This is because Tstat does not recognized obfuscated eDonkey traffic.

Table 1. Tstat vs. Claude comparison

Tstat 2.0 vs Claude [%]			
Class	Tstat Breakdown	Claude Breakdown	Overlap
UNKNOWN	32,67	12	27,92
WEB	58,35	77	81,31
EDONKEY	3,81	4,85	90,72
BITTORENT	0,91	1,06	99,52
ARES	0,09	0,06	99,53
MAIL	3,65	5,06	83,41

We fed Tstat with hand-made obfuscated eDonkey traces to confirm that it does not detect encrypted traffic.

The main lesson we learn from the above study is that even two state-of-the-art DPI tools can lead to sometimes significantly different reference points. We leave the detailed investigation of the root cause of those differences as further work. In the remaining of this paper, we rely on Claude only, due to the lowest fraction of the Unknown traffic it offers and the largest variety of the applications that the tool can handle, as compared to Tstat.

4 Trace

For our tests we use an ADSL trace captured in 2008. The trace was collected using passive probes located just behind the so-called Broadband Access Server. The capture was performed without any sampling or loss. The trace contains one hour full bidirectional traffic of 3237 end users of the ADSL platform. The whole payload is available along with packet headers. A short description of the trace is provided in Table 2. In this work we consider TCP traffic only as it is the dominating transport layer. All the IPs except for the Unknown class flows were fully anonymized. Traffic was classified with Claude.

We consider two levels of traffic class division. First, a less detailed division containing: Web, Streaming, P2P, Mail, Ftp, Others, Chat, Games, Database. Second, a richer set where the p2p class is further divided into several popular applications, namely eMule , Bittorrent , Gnutella , Ares, TribalWeb and other applications. In the second set, we also divide the Streaming class into p2p Streaming and http Streaming. Not all of the applications that our classification tool is capable of detecting are present in the set. Breakdown of flows and bytes for the trace is given in Figures 1(a), 1(b). Figure 2(d) depicts a more detailed breakdown of peer-to-peer applications. Our data set contains a large fraction of Web traffic, which accounts for more than half of the bytes and over 70% of flows. Concerning the bytes transferred, the second class is Streaming which transfers even more data than the p2p class. As for the p2p class, most bytes and flows are generated due to eDonkey followed by Bittorent. Among the less popular applications, we observed only Gnutella and Ares. The fraction of Unknown flows, which our refference point tool was not able to classify, is 11%.

Table 2. Trace summary

Data set	Date	Start time	Duration [h]	Size [GB]	Packets	TCP Flows
MS-I	2008-02-04	14:45	1	26	47'616'695	626'727

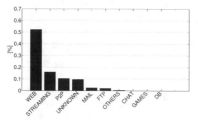

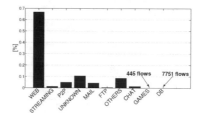

(a) Application breakdown. Bytes.   (b) Application breakdown. Flows.

Fig. 1.

5   Machine Learning Classification

In this section, we report on our experience with machine learning techniques and different sets of application classes. We used the same flow feature to perform the classification for both levels of precision. Those were extracted using an internal tool providing over eighty per flow features and ad-hoc scripts to obtain other discriminators. We tested several supervised algorithms (Naive Bayes with Kernel estimation, Bayesian Network, Support Vector Machine and C4.5) and features sets in order to find the best performing one. For all the algorithms, we used the WEKA suite [10] that is a machine learning toolkit implementing a variety of state of the art methods for data mining. We selected the following per flow features: inter packet time (up and down), mean packet size (up and down), number of pushed packets (up/down), number of data packets. Using this set, we tested several supervised classification algorithms in order to find the one offering the best overall accuracy for our case. The best performance in terms of accuracy and speed were provided by the C4.5 decision tree algorithm. Those results are in line with the ones in [7], where C4.5 appeared also to be the fastest algorithm with a good (but not the best) accuracy.

We applied the widely used method called N-fold cross validation to train the tool [8]. The dataset is randomly split into N parts. Each part is used for training, while the rest is used for testing the accuracy. The process is repeated N times and the resulting performance measures are averaged across all the experiments. We used N=10, as it was claimed in [8] that this number provides a good approximation of operational performance.

The overall accuracy, defined as the fraction of correctly classified flows over all class is 96.62% for the general application breakdown using C.4.5. However, the overall accuracy can be misleading, as classes of traffic are not equally represented in the set. In Figure 2(a) we depict per class accuracy and precision. For most classes we get reasonable accuracy varying between 65% for the DB class to 98% for Web. Streaming

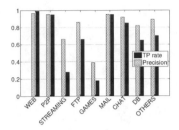

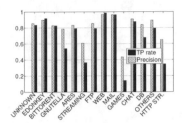

(a) Per application TP rate and precision

(b) Per application TP rate and precision. Detailed grained classes definition.

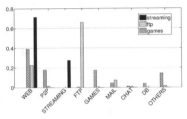

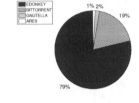

(c) Miss classification results

(d) Application breakdown inside peer-to-peer class. Flows.

Fig. 2.

and Games achieved very poor TP rate, but reasonable precision. This means that although a large fraction of Streaming and Games flows are misclassified, flows classified as beeing in those classes are actually belonging to them. In order to better understand the misclassification problem, we present in Figure 2(c) the relative confusion matrix for the applications classes that performed poorly. Streaming is misclassified almost each time as Web traffic. A significant fraction of Ftp flows falls also into this class. For Games, flows are spread mainly over Web, P2P and Others classes. This result suggests that additional features should be used to better discriminate the poorly performing traffic types.

For the case of the more detailed application breakdown, the overall accuracy remains as high as 94.77%. As a result, we get very promising per class performance for most cases. The four p2p applications are well separated. The best accuracy is obtained for eDonkey: 95% and the worst one for Gnutella (50%). Bittorent and Ares have reasonable accuracy, around 80%. As we used the same features set and algorithm as in the previous step, the problem of Streaming and Games still remains. As for the confusion matrix for p2p applications, Gnutella flows fall mainly into the Bittorent class, whereas Bittorrent itself, is well classified. For both applications, the misclassified flows fall into non p2p classes.

This section aimed at pinpointing the need to tune the classification technique (one could change the algorithm or the flow features) to be used depending on the level of granularity and also on the application one wants to focus on. The confusion matrix appears to be a valuable tool in the tuning phase.

6 Mining the Unknown Class

We now focus on mining the unknown class, which was not classified by our reference tool. We first calibrated our statistical classifier using the flows classified by our DPI tool and then used it to the flows labeled as Unknown. Our algorithm outputs for every flow a prediction of class along with a probability of correct classification. We use the following heuristic to interpret results. If the prediction probability is higher or equal to a given threshold we assume the predicted class is correct. Otherwise we assume that the confidence is to low, so the flow remains unknown. Figure 3 depicts the cumulative distribution function of per flow confidence levels of classification for the unknown class. From the curve we can read what fraction of the flows can be classified assuming a specific confidence threshold. We test 2 threshold levels: 0.95 and 0.99. In this way, we are able to give insights about probable applications types generating unknown traffic. Results are provided in Table 3. Depending on the threshold, we are able to reveal between 50% and 63% of the unknown flows. Assuming a strict confidence level of 0.99, we are able to reduce the number of unknown flows by a factor of 2. Classified flows in our unknown class are mainly eDonkey and Web flows.

For the unknown flows case, we lack the reference point, so we are not able to directly assess the actual accuracy of the method proposed. However, we performed several side analyzes aiming to challenge the statistical predictions. We leverage the fact that we have the IP addresses and used port numbers of the endpoints of our flows. We perform the following tests:

- Reverse DNS lookup for each remote endpoint: We parse the answer, searching for meaningful keywords.
- For each flow classified as Web, we tested if there was indeed a Web server. We used wget service.
- Look for unknown remote endpoints in the known set: if a flow concerning this endpoint was once classified, e.g. eDonkey, other connections concerning same endpoint are very likely to be of similar type.

For the DNS lookup test, we obtained 79% of answers. In many cases, the host name can be meaningful. For example, many providers indicate in the host name that it is an ADSL host. Also searching for known ADSL providers names in the domains helps identifying home users[2]. Almost all end hosts, for flows predicted as p2p are ADSL hosts which seems to confirm the results of the classifier. What is more, we observe a large fraction of legacy ports of eDonkey or its simple variations in this set. Trying to connect using **wget** to endpoints for flows predicted to be Web, we obtained answers for only 7 % of the hosts, usually with https services, e.g., login pages of webmails. This explains why the ground truth tool failed in these cases. Looking at DNS resolutions of these endpoints, we observe a large fraction of home users rather than typical Web servers. It is hard to believe that home users were running so many Web services at the time of the capture. Given the results in Figure 2(c), it is very probable that a large

---

[2] We use keywords: "DSL", "wanadoo", "free.fr", "club-internet" (popular french ADSL providers). We also check for specific operators hostname syntax to aviod confusion with providers website adress.

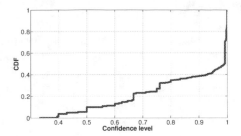

Fig. 3. CDF of fraction of flows classified depending on confidence level

Table 3. Unknown class predictions from C4.5

Unknown class predictions			
Confidence	0.95	Confidence	0.99
Class	[%]	Class	[%]
EDONKEY	23.07	EDONKEY	21.75
WEB	21.54	WEB	18.09
OTHERS	5.06	OTHERS	4.39
CHAT	1.75	CHAT	1.63
MAIL	1.69	GAMES	1.50
BITTORRENT	1.67	MAIL	1.07
GAMES	1.50	BITTORRENT	0.96
DB	0.56	DB	0.55
FTP	0.41	FTP	0.29
ARES	0.01	ARES	0.01
SUM	57.26	SUM	50.24

fraction of predictions for Web traffic are misclassified Streaming applications. What is more, the large fraction of Streaming in the known set consists of http Streaming. This explains why this traffic is statistically close to Web. Finally, for each endpoint in the unknown set, we look if it was present among the known flows. Only 18% of the unknown endpoints were present in the classified set, so it is not enough to draw overall conclusions. Endpoints identified contains mainly eDonkey users hosts. The method could work well if we had a larger users set, resulting in possibly larger fraction of the remote endpoints identified.

As a conclusion, except for the Web class our predictions are backed up by endpoints profiling. We might need a more precise classification method for Streaming application in order to provide more reliable predictions for the unknown class.

7   Discussion

In this paper, we have highlighted some key issues that arise when using statistical traffic classification tools. We have compared the outcomes provided by three different DPI tools. This comparison underscores the difficulty of assessing the results of any statistical tool as the accuracy it achieves is partly correlated to the quality of the DPI tool used to establish the reference point. Reference point establishment is in fact a complex task and a good understanding of the design choices (e.g., Is http streaming classified as Streaming or Web?) is necessary to interpret the result.

We also shown that the exact level granularity that is requested might require changes in the method in terms of classification algorithm or flow features. From a methodological point of view, the confusion matrix turns out to provide a simple way of pinpointing the defaults of a classification method.

Last but not least, we have focused on the problem of mining flows classified as unknown by the DPI tool. We have shown how to take advantage of the confidence level provided by the classification algorithm to control the accuracy of the classification. We further demonstrated that simple heuristics could further back the results of the classifier and overcome the lack of reference point in this case.

References

1. Trestian, I., Ranjan, S., Kuzmanovic, A., Nucci, A.: Unconstrained Endpoint Profiling (Googling the Internet). In: Proceedings of ACM SIGCOMM 2008, Seattle, WA (August 2008)
2. Bernaille, L., Teixeira, R., Salamatian, K.: Early Application Identification. In: The 2nd ADETTI/ISCTE CoNEXT Conference, Lisboa, Portugal (December 2006)
3. Erman, M.A., Mahanti, A.: Traffic Classification Using Clustering Algorithms. In: Proceedings of the 2006 SIGCOMM workshop on Mining network data, Pisa (Italy), September 2006, pp. 281–286 (2006)
4. Dreder, H., Feldmann, A., Paxson, V., Sommer, R.: Operational Experiences with High-Volume Network Intrusion Detection. In: Proceedings of the 11th ACM conference on Computer and communications security, Washington DC, USA (2004)
5. Szabo, G., Orincsay, D., Malomsoky, S., Szabó, I.: On the Validation of Traffic Classification Algorithms. In: Claypool, M., Uhlig, S. (eds.) PAM 2008. LNCS, vol. 4979, pp. 72–81. Springer, Heidelberg (2008)
6. Paxson, V.: Empirically derived analytic models of wide-area TCP connections. IEEE/ACM Transactions on Networking 2(4), 316–336 (1994)
7. Kim, H., Claffy, K.C., Fomenkova, M., Barman, D., Faloutsos, M., Lee, K.Y.: Internet Traffic Classificatoin Demystified: Myths, Caveats, and the Best Practices. In: ACM CoNEXT, Madrid, Spain (December 2008)
8. Nguyen, T.T.T., Armitage, G.: A Survey of Techniques for Internet Traffic Classification using Machine Learning. In: IEEE Communications Surveys Tutorials, 4th edn. (2008)
9. Bro, http://www.bro-ids.org/
10. WEKA data mining, http://www.cs.waikato.ac.nz/ml/weka/
11. Tstat, http://tstat.tlc.polito.it/

Accurate, Fine-Grained Classification of P2P-TV Applications by Simply Counting Packets

Silvio Valenti[1], Dario Rossi[1], Michela Meo[2], Marco Mellia[2], and Paola Bermolen[1]

[1] TELECOM ParisTech, France
first.last@telecom-paristech.fr
[2] Politecnico di Torino, Italy
first.last@polito.it

Abstract. We present a novel methodology to accurately classify the traffic generated by P2P-TV applications, relying only on the count of packets they exchange with other peers during small time-windows. The rationale is that even a raw count of exchanged packets conveys a wealth of useful information concerning several implementation aspects of a P2P-TV application – such as network discovery and signaling activities, video content distribution and chunk size, etc. By validating our framework, which makes use of Support Vector Machines, on a large set of P2P-TV testbed traces, we show that it is actually possible to reliably discriminate among different applications by simply counting packets.

1 Introduction

The Internet proved to have an amazing capability of adapting to new services, migrating from the initial pure datagram paradigm to a real multi-service infrastructure. One of the most recent steps of this evolution is constituted by P2P-TV, i.e., large-scale real-time video-streaming services which exploit the peer-to-peer communication paradigm, and already count millions of users worldwide.

As such, the identification of P2P-TV applications is a topic of undoubted interest, which has not been addressed yet, despite the valuable effort already devoted to the task of traffic classification [1, 2, 3, 4, 5, 6, 7, 8, 9]. In this field *behavioral classification* [1, 2] is a novel approach which aims at identifying the traffic generated by network hosts or end-points by the sole examination of their traffic patterns (e.g. number of hosts contacted, transport layer protocol employed, number of different ports used, etc.). This approach is very light-weight, as it requires neither the inspection of packet payload as in [3, 4], nor operations on a per-packet basis as in [7, 8]. However, so far, behavioral classification has been able only to discriminate broad application *classes* (e.g., interactive, P2P, Web, etc.) rather than different applications *within* the same class.

This work is the first to propose a *fine-grained* classification engine which only exploits behavioral characteristics – namely, the count of packets exchanged by peers during small time-windows. Our framework, which is tailored for P2P-TV applications such as PPLive, SopCast, TVAnts and Joost[1], makes use of the Support Vector Machines. We validate the engine by means of a large and diverse set of traces collected

---

[1] Since October 2008 Joost is no more using P2P to deliver video content.

M. Papadopouli, P. Owezarski, and A. Pras (Eds.): TMA 2009, LNCS 5537, pp. 84–92, 2009.

over a pan-European testbed: experimental results show that it is possible to discriminate among different P2P-TV applications by simply counting packets – as true positive classification accounts to more than 81% of packets, bytes and peers in the *worst case*.

2 Classification Framework

The Rationale
Our aim is to classify P2P-TV end-points, identified by a network address and transport layer port pair $(IP, port)$. Typically, a P2P-TV application running on a given IP host multiplexes signaling and video traffic exchanged with other peers on a single port. We assume our engine to be situated at the *edge* of the network, where all the traffic exchanged by a given end-point transits. Furthermore, we restrict our attention to UDP traffic only, as it is the transport layer protocol preferred by P2P-TV applications.

Since UDP is a connectionless transport protocol, we cannot exploit any kind of flow semantic to perform the classification. As such, we rely solely on the count of packets a P2P-TV application exchanges with other peers during small time-windows. Indeed, we advocate that application *signatures* based on the raw packet count convey a wealth of useful information, tied to several design aspects of an application (i.e., overlay discovery and signaling activities, video diffusion policy, etc.).

A human analogy may help in clarifying this intuition. Let us compare peers in the network to people in a party room: human beings have rather different attitudes and behaviors, just as peers do. For instance, somebody prefers lengthy talks with a few friends: similarly, some application tends to keep exchanging data with the same peers as long as possible. Somebody else, on the contrary, may prefer to briefly chat with a lot of people, just like applications with an intense network discovery activity and a dynamic diffusion of the video content would do.

Furthermore P2P-TV applications exchange the video stream in *chunks*, i.e., minimum units of data with a fixed length, that are thus transferred with the same number of packets: since each application independently selects its own chunk size, differences in this choice will be reflected by the raw packet count.

Finally, in the following we consider only the downlink traffic direction. Indeed, we point out that P2P-TV applications need a rather steady downlink throughput to ensure a smooth playback: in fact, it has been observed that while peers *consume* equally, they do not *contribute* equally [11] to the video diffusion. Therefore, we expect the downlink traffic direction alone to convey all the needed information for a correct classification.

Behavioral P2P-TV Signature
More formally, let us consider the traffic received by an end-point $\mathcal{P}_x = (IP_x, port_x)$ during an interval ΔT, which, for the remainder of this work, we fix to $\Delta T = 5$ seconds. During this interval, peer $\mathcal{P}_x$ will be contacted by $K(x)$ other peers, namely $\mathcal{P}_1 \ldots \mathcal{P}_{K(x)}$, receiving a different number of packets from each of them, say $p_1 \ldots p_{K(x)}$. Then, we derive the number N_I^x of peers that sent a number of packets in an interval $I = [a, b]$ to peer $\mathcal{P}_x$ i.e. denoting with $\mathbf{1}\{\cdot\}$ is the indicator function:

$$N_I^x = \sum_{j=1}^{K(x)} \mathbf{1}\{p_j \in I\} \tag{1}$$

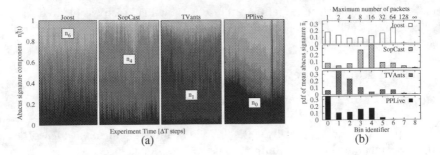

Fig. 1. Abacus signatures of P2P-TV application: (a) temporal evolution and (b) mean value

In particular we use $B + 1$ intervals of exponential width $\{I_0, \ldots, I_i, \ldots, I_B\}$ such that $I_0 = (0, 1]$, $I_i = (2^{i-1}, 2^i]$, and $I_B = (2^B, \infty]$. In other words, $N_i^x = N_{I_i}^x$ will count the number of peers sending to $\mathcal{P}_x$ a number of packets in the interval $(2^{i-1}, 2^i]$, while $N_B^x = N_{I_B}^x$ will count all peers sending at least 2^B packets to $\mathcal{P}_x$. As previously explained, we expect that if the application performs network discovery by means of single packet probes and uses $C = 16$ packet long chunks, there will be a large number of peers falling into the N_0^x and N_4^x bins. For each time interval ΔT, we then build a behavioral signature $\underline{n}^x = (n_0^x, \ldots, n_B^x) \in \mathbb{R}^{B+1}$, by normalizing N_i^x over the total number $K(x)$ of peers that contacted $\mathcal{P}_x$ during that interval:

$$n_i^x = \frac{N_i^x}{\sum_{b=0}^B N_b^x} = \frac{N_i^x}{K(x)}, \quad \text{and} \quad |\underline{n}^x| = \sum_{i=0}^B n_i^x = 1 \qquad (2)$$

Since signature $\underline{n}^x$ has been derived from a pure count of the number of exchanged packets, we name it *abacus* (shorthand for "automated behavioral application classification using signatures"). An example of the temporal evolution of abacus signatures $\underline{n}^x(t)$ is given in Fig. 1-(a). considering the behavior of an arbitrary peer $\mathcal{P}_x$ during 1-hour long experiment for the four different applications. Time of the experiment runs on the x-axis in multiples of ΔT, whereas y-axis reports the *cumulative* abacus signature, using different fading colors for different bins. Bins are ordered from bottom to top, so that bin number 0 (which is the darkest one), starts at the bottom of the y-axis scale and extends until n_0^x. Subsequent bins are then *incrementally* staggered (with progressively lighter colors), so that the k-th bin starts at $\sum_{i=0}^{k-1} n_i^x$ and the last bin extends until $|\underline{n}^x| = 1$.

Already at a first glance, we notice that for any given application one bin (which is labeled in the picture) is remarkably wider than the others. Moreover, while the widest bin differs across applications, it keeps roughly the same for any given application, during most of the experiment duration, despite its actual width changes over time. This can be more easily gathered by comparing the *mean* per-application signature, averaged over all time intervals, reported in Fig. 1-(b). for instance, during a 5-seconds interval, Joost peers tend to exchange either a single or several (33–64) packets to any given peer, whereas SopCast performs less probing sending also fewer (9–16) packets.

TVants prefers instead lower order bins (2–4 packets), and PPLive makes a significant use of single packet exchanges, possibly to discover the network, while the rest of its activity is more spread out over the other bins.

Support Vector Machines

Our classification framework makes use of Support Vector Machines (SVMs) [10], which are well known among the *supervised* learning methods for their discriminative power. In SVM, entities to be classified are represented by means of some distinctive "features", i.e., the abacus signatures in our case. SVM classification is a two-phase process. First, SVM needs to be trained with supervised input (i.e., abacus signatures of known traffic and the corresponding application label). The output of this phase is a model, which can then be applied in a second phase to classify previously unseen signatures.

Given a geometric representation of features in a multi-dimensional space, the training phase partitions the feature space into a set of classes, using a few representative samples of each class. Then, during the classification phase, any new point is assigned to the most likely class, depending on the zone the point falls into. Defining the delimiting surfaces is complex, since training points can be spread out on the feature space: the key idea of SVM is to remap the original space into a higher dimensional one, so that different classes can be separated by the simplest surfaces, i.e., hyper-planes. To assess the classification results, signatures are computed over known validation traffic (different from the one used in the training phase), and are then fed to SVM model: finally, classification results are compared with the real label.

Rejection Criterion

An important point is that, since SVM induces a *partition* on the abacus feature space, any new point is necessarily labeled as one of the applications offered to SVM during the training phase. Since we trained our machine only with P2P-TV traffic, any unknown application would be mistakenly classified as P2P-TV. Therefore, in order to have an effective classification engine, we need to define a *rejection criterion*.

Given two probability density functions, there exist several indexes to evaluate their similarity. The Bhattacharyya distance BD [12] is a measure of the divergence of two pdfs, which verifies the triangular inequality. In the case of two discrete probability p and q in $\mathbb{R}^n$, it is defined by:

$$BD(p,q) = \sqrt{1 - B} \quad \text{where} \quad B = \sum_{k=1}^{n} \sqrt{(p(k) * q(k))} \tag{3}$$

B is known as Bhattacharyya coefficient and $0 \leq B \leq 1$. Values of BD near to zero indicates strong similarity (if $p(k) = q(k) \quad \forall k$, $B = 1$ and $BD = 0$) whereas values near to one indicates weak similarity.

In our context we *reject* the SVM classification label C of a sample signature n whenever the distance $BD(n, \overline{n}(C))$ exceeds a given threshold R, where $\overline{n}(C)$ is the average signature computed over all training set signatures of application C. In other words, we accept the SVM decision only if the signature n lies within a radius R from the center of the SVM training set for that class. Otherwise we label the signature sample as "unknown". For the time being we set $R = 0.5$ and discuss the impact of this choice, as well as its motivation, later on.

3   Experimental Results

Testbed setup

Assessing traffic classification performance is known not to be a trivial task due to the difficulty to devise a reliable "oracle" to known the "ground truth", i.e., what was the actual application that generated the traffic [4]. Testing the classification engine by means of artificial traffic (e.g., by generating traffic in a testbed) solves the problem of knowing the ground truth (i.e., you are the oracle), but care must be taken in order to ensure testbed traces to be representative of real world traffic.

Therefore, to overcome this issue, we setup a large testbed in the context of NAPA-WINE, a 7th Framework Programme project funded by the EU [13], whose main features are summarized in Tab. 1. Partners took part in the experiments by running P2P-TV clients on PCs connected either to the institution LAN, or to home networks having cable/DSL access. In more detail, the setup involved a total of 44 peers, including 37 PCs from 7 different industrial/academic sites, and 7 home PCs. Probes are distributed over four countries, and connected to 6 different Autonomous Systems, while home PCs are connected to 7 other ASs and ISPs. Moreover, different experiments and peers configurations (hardware, OS version, channel popularity, etc.) further ensure that the testbed is representative of a wide range of scenarios. We considered four different applications, namely PPLive, SopCast, TVAnts and Joost and we performed several 1-hour long experiments during April 2008, where partners watched the same channel at the same time and collected packet-level traces. In all cases, the nominal stream rate was 384kbps. Overall, the testbed dataset amounts to about 5.5 days worth of video streaming, $100 \cdot 10^3$ signatures samples, $48 \cdot 10^6$ packets, 26 GBytes of data.

In order to asses the ability of our system to correctly label as unknown the traffic generated by non P2P-TV applications, we also collected packet level traces from our campus network. Particularly we isolated the traffic generated by two widely adopted P2P applications, i.e. Skype and eDonkey as examples of respectively P2P voice and file-sharing applications. To identify eDonkey we employed a DPI classifier based on [14], while for Skype we resorted to [9]. The final dataset amounts to about 2.2GBytes and 1,4GBytes of data for Skype and eDonkey respectively, which correspond to $500 \cdot 10^3$ and $300 \cdot 10^3$ signatures.

Discriminating P2P-TV applications

We use the signatures extracted from the testbed traffic to assess the ability of the engine to reveal P2P-TV traffic and to distinguish the different applications. Numerical results reported in the following are obtained by training the SVM with 20% of the testbed signatures selected at random, and using the remaining 80% for validation. Experiments are then repeated 10 times, randomizing the training set each time, so to gather robust results. Performance are expressed in terms of the amount of True Positive (TP, i.e. classifying label X correctly as X), and False Negative (FN, i.e. labelling a X sample as Y) classifications, and by measuring the TP-Rate (TPR) or *recall*, defined as TPR=TP/(TP+FN).

Table 1. Summary of the hosts, sites, countries (CC), autonomous systems (AS) and access types of the peers involved in the experiments

Host	Site	CC	AS	Access	Nat	FW	Host	Site	CC	AS	Access	Nat	FW
1-4	BME	HU	AS1	high-bw	-	-	1-4	ENST	FR	AS4	high-bw	-	Y
5			ASx	DSL 6/0.512	-	-	5			ASx	DSL 22/1.8	Y	-
1-9	PoliTO	IT	AS2	high-bw	-	-	1-5	UniTN	IT	AS2	high-bw	-	-
10			ASx	DSL 4/0.384	-	-	6-7				high-bw	Y	-
11-12			ASx	DSL 8/0.384	Y	-	8			ASx	DSL 2.5/0.384	Y	Y
1-4	MT	HU	AS3	high-bw	-	-	1-8	WUT	PL	AS6	high-bw	-	-
1-3	FFT	FR	AS5	high-bw	-	-	9			ASx	CATV 6/0.512	-	-

Table 2. Confusion matrix of P2P-TV application (left table) and per signature, packets, bytes and end-point classification results (right table)

	Signatures: Confusion Matrix					Signatures			Packets			Bytes			Peer	
	PPLive	TVants	SopCast	Joost	Unk	TP	Mis	Unk	TP	Mis	Unk	TP	Mis	Unk	TP	Unk (n)
PPLive	81.66	0.58	9.55	2.32	5.90	81.7	12.4	5.9	91.3	8.7	0.0	91.6	8.4	0.0	96.2	3.8 (1)
TVants	0.41	98.84	0.15	0.57	0.04	98.8	1.2	0.0	99.6	0.3	0.1	99.6	0.3	0.1	100	0 (0)
SopCast	3.76	0.11	89.62	0.32	6.19	89.6	4.2	6.2	94.7	1.7	3.6	94.0	1.8	4.2	94.4	5.6 (2)
Joost	2.84	0.55	0.28	89.47	6.86	89.5	3.7	6.8	92.1	2.3	5.6	92.2	2.4	5.4	93.3	6.6 (2)

Let us start by observing the left part of Tab. 2, which reports the classification performance relative to individual end-point signatures samples, corresponding to $\Delta T = 5$ s. worth of traffic, adopting a "confusion matrix" representation. For each row, testbed traffic signatures are classified using SVM and the classification result is reported in different columns. Diagonals of the matrix correspond to correct classification TPR, whereas elements outside the diagonal correspond to FN misclassification. Particularly the last column reports the traffic which is classified as "unknown" by the rejection criterion. It can be seen that, in the worst case, individual signatures are correctly classified nearly the 82% of the times. The application most difficult to identify appears to be PPLive, which generates 9.6% of SopCast False Positives, while for the all others the TP percentage exceeds 89%. All applications but TVAnts generate about 6% of "unknown" false negative (i.e. rejected due to a large BD distance.)

We next quantify the classification performance also in terms of the number of correctly classified *packets*, *bytes* and *peers*. In more detail, to each signature a precise number of packets and bytes directly corresponds, so that the per-packets and per-byte metrics can be directly evaluated. In the case of per-peer classification, we instead combine several classification decisions, and evaluate whether the *majority* of signature samples for a given end-point has been correctly classified over its whole 1-hour long experiment. We point out that, while the classification engine is able to take a decision "early" (more precisely, after a delay of ΔT seconds), in the latter case of end-point classification we actually need *all* observations of a given experiment, falling therefore in the context of "late" classification. Right portion of Tab. 2 reports the percentage of correct classification (TPR), of misclassification (Mis, corresponding to the sum of row values that fall outside of the diagonal in the confusion matrix) and rejection (Unk) in terms of signature, packets, bytes and peer metrics; notice that FN=Mis+Unk.

Interestingly, we see that performance improves for all applications, and especially for PPLive, when considering *packets* and *bytes* metrics with respect to *signature*

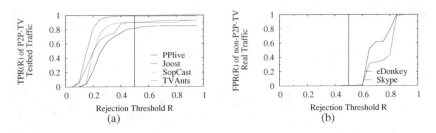

Fig. 2. TPR of P2P-TV (a) and FPR of non-P2P-TV (b) as a function of the rejection threshold R

samples: this means that misclassification happens when fewer packets/bytes are received (i.e., when the application is possibly mal-functioning). In case of end-point classification, reliability slightly increases, as the recall for all applications is greater than 93%. While results are more than satisfactory, yet we observe that identification of some peer fails even in the case of late classification, with a total of 5 tests classified as unknown, as highlighted in the last column of the table. Digging further we actually found that mainly 3 hosts are responsible for the misclassification, and moreover all of them actually showed abnormal functioning during the experiments.

Classifying the Unknown
If the rejection criterion generates about 5% of additional false negatives for the classification of P2P-TV applications, it reveals to be very effective in correctly handling unknown applications. In fact for both Skype and eDonkey traces our engine raises only 0.1% of false alarms: in other words, only 0.1% of the signature samples are not label as "unknown" as they should, but are rather labeled as one of the P2P-TV applications.

Results early shown highly depend on the rejection threshold R, whose choice depends on the following tradeoff. Intuitively, R should be as large as possible, to avoid classifying P2P-TV as Unknown (i.e., maximize the TPR) but, at the same time, R should be as small as possible to avoid classifying irrelevant traffic as P2P-TV (i.e., minimize the false positive rate, FPR). To validate the choice of $R = 0.5$ we proceeded as follows. Using testbed traces, we empirically evaluate the TPR as a function of the rejection threshold R, which is depicted in Fig. 2-(a). It can be seen that TPR quickly saturates, meaning that no P2P-TV signature is rejected when $R \geq 0.5$. We then use the non-P2P-TV traffic from our campus network to instead evaluate the FPR as a function of R, shown in Fig. 2-(b). In this case, due to the partitioning approach of SVM, eDonkey and Skype signatures are forcibly labeled by SVM as one of the P2P-TV applications: however, the BD distance of the labeled signature from the center of the cluster is likely higher than that of a true P2P-TV application. This clearly emerges from Fig. 2-(b), which show that for low values of $R \leq 0.5$, practically no false alarm is raised.

We specify that these are preliminary results, and that we plan to test the effectiveness of the rejection criterion on a wider range of non P2P-TV protocols as a future work. Yet, we showed that our rejection mechanism can correctly handle two widely used applications, representative of two different families of P2P protocols, by successfully identify them as unknown.

4   Conclusions

This work proposed a novel technique for the classification of P2P-TV applications, which relies on the count of packets exchanged amongst peers during small time-windows, and makes use of Support Vector Machines.

Through measurement collected in a large testbed, we show that our classification engine, is able to correctly classify more than 81% of signatures in the worst case. If performance is evaluated considering packets, bytes or peers metrics, correct classifications amount to 91% in the worst case. Moreover the rejection criterion we designed is able to correctly handle unknown applications, raising only 0.1% of false alarms.

We believe this work to be a first step toward accurate, fine-grained, behavioral classification: several aspects remains indeed uncovered (e.g., byte-wise vs packet-wise signatures, more P2P applications, TCP traffic, training set selection etc.), which we plan to address in the future.

Acknowledgements

This work was funded by EU under the FP7 Collaborative Project "Network-Aware P2P-TV Applications over Wise-Networks" (NAPAWINE).

References

1. Karagiannis, T., Papagiannaki, K., Faloutsos, M.: BLINC: multilevel traffic classification in the dark. ACM Communication Review 35(4) (2005)
2. Xu, K., Zhang, Z., Bhattacharyya, S.: Profiling internet backbone traffic: behavior models and applications. In: ACM SIGCOMM 2005, Philadelphia, PA, August 2005, pp. 169–180 (2005)
3. Sen, S., Spatscheck, O., Wang, D.: Accurate, scalable in-network identification of p2p traffic using application signatures. In: WWW 2004, NY (May 2004)
4. Moore, A.W., Papagiannaki, K.: Toward the Accurate Identification of Network Applications. In: Dovrolis, C. (ed.) PAM 2005. LNCS, vol. 3431, pp. 41–54. Springer, Heidelberg (2005)
5. Roughan, M., Sen, S., Spatscheck, O., Duffield, N.: Class-of-service mapping for QoS: a statistical signature-based approach to IP traffic classification. In: ACM IMC 2004 (October 2004)
6. Moore, A.W., Zuev, D.: Internet traffic classification using bayesian analysis techniques. In: ACM SIGMETRICS 2005 (2005)
7. Bernaille, L., Teixeira, R., Salamatian, K.: Early Application Identification. In: Conference on Future Networking Technologies (CoNEXT 2006), Lisboa, PT (December 2006)
8. Crotti, M., Dusi, M., Gringoli, F., Salgarelli, L.: Traffic Classification through Simple Statistical Fingerprinting. ACM Computer Communication Review 37(1) (January 2007)
9. Bonfiglio, D., Mellia, M., Meo, M., Rossi, D., Tofanelli, P.: Revealing Skype Traffic: when Randomness Plays with You. In: ACM SIGCOMM, Kyoto, Japan (August 2007)

10. Cristianini, N., Shawe-Taylor, J.: An introduction to support Vector Machines and other kernel-based learning methods. Cambridge University Press, New York (1999)
11. Hei, X., Liang, C., Liang, J., Liu, Y., Ross, K.W.: A Measurement Study of a Large-Scale P2P IPTV System. In: IEEE Transactions on Multimedia (December 2007)
12. Bhattacharyya, A.: On a measure of divergence between two statistical populations defined by probability distributions. Bull. Calcutta Math. Soc. 35, 99–109 (1943)
13. NAPA-WINE, http://www.napa-wine.eu
14. Kulbak, Y., Bickson, D.: The eMule protocol specification. Tech. Rep. Leibniz Center TR-2005-03 (2005)

Detection and Tracking of Skype by Exploiting Cross Layer Information in a Live 3G Network

Philipp Svoboda[1], Esa Hyytiä[2], Fabio Ricciato[2],
Markus Rupp[1], and Martin Karner[3]

[1] INTHFT Department, Vienna University of Technology, Vienna, Austria
[2] Forschungszentrum Telekommunikation Wien, Vienna, Austria
[3] mobilkom austria AG, Vienna, Austria

Abstract. This paper introduces a new method to detect and track Skype traffic and users by exploiting cross layer information available within 3G mobile cellular networks. In a 3G core network all flows can be analyzed on a per user basis. A detected Skype message is therefore related to a specific user. This information enables user profiles that provide a relationship between the mobile station and the characteristics of the corresponding Skype instance, which remain unchanged for long periods of time. Based on this information, our computationally lightweight method is able to classify Skype flows accurately. Moreover, the method is, by design, robust against false positives. Based on test traces from a live network, our new method achieves a similar detection performance as publicly available tools, yet with much less complexity.

1 Introduction

Nowadays, 2009, the traffic in the packet switched domain is increasing fast. Therefore, the operators are interested which services are present in the PS domain and as a next step how to optimize the network accordingly. In previous studies we classified traffic based on the port numbers found in the traffic flows. However, over the time the share of traffic we could identify reliably has started to decrease. In addition to this, we want to be able to discriminate background noise originated from Skype nodes probing for other nodes from port scans and attacks against the network elements [1]. Therefore, we have started to research in more advanced traffic classification for the traces from the measured 3G core network.

In this work we focus on the detection of Skype traffic in a 3G core network. The core network of a mobile operator offers various additional signaling information, which can be used to analyze traffic of each user. More specifically, the signaling information relates each IP packet with a mobile host, and therefore with a specific user or mobile station (MS). Our approach is different from other studies, and is in some sense more practical, as the major part of the work takes place when the signaling traffic is analyzed. Note that we gain here as the signaling load represents only a small fraction of the flow arrival rate. After that, the classification of an individual data flow translates to a simple query from a user profile database.

M. Papadopouli, P. Owezarski, and A. Pras (Eds.): TMA 2009, LNCS 5537, pp. 93–100, 2009.
© Springer-Verlag Berlin Heidelberg 2009

Several methods to detect Skype traffic on a network link have been proposed [2–4]. The first method [2] is similar to our approach, but for Internet backbone links. In fact, our focus is not in traffic classification, but in the user satisfaction with the service Skype. The presence of a Skype user is detected via a call to the update server. The Skype port is then set to the most active UDP port.

The second method [3], and its advanced implementations [4], are based on statistical classification. Firstly, a voice communication has certain unique characteristics and, therefore, VoIP flows will have, e.g., a constant rate and small packet size. Secondly, Skype packets have certain structure, and the classifier can check that the first two byte and the data area have a high entropy, as they are encrypted, and that the third byte has a low entropy, as it is signaling.

Our method is combining well known facts from the other papers to gather information on Skype traffic. However, to the best of our knowledge, the particular idea to store in a central database information on the services a user accesses and the settings the client of the user, as discussed in the paper have not been proposed in the literature.

2   Measurement Setup

The reference network scenario is depicted in Fig. 1. As most access networks, the 3G mobile network has a hierarchical tree-like deployment. The mobile stations and base stations are geographically distributed. Going up in the hierarchy (see [5]) the level of concentration increases, involving a progressively smaller number of equipments and physical sites. In a typical network there are relatively few Serving GPRS Support Nodes (SGSN) and even fewer Gateway GPRS Support port Nodes (GGSN). Therefore it is possible to capture the whole data traffic from home subscribers on a small number of Gn/Gi links. For further details on the structure of a 3G mobile network refer to [5].

Measurement System: We used the monitoring system described in [6]. This system supports all protocols of the packet switched domain in a 3G core network, MS tracking per packet, and user mobility. Independent modules, so called metrics, can be attached to this system working with the derived data sets. The measurement modules run online to avoid the storage of user critical payload data. To meet privacy requirements traces are anonymized by replacing all fields related to user identity at the lower 3G layers with unique identifiers which cannot be reversed, while the user payload above the TCP/IP layer is removed after the checking. Therefore, our system is able to associate packets and to reconstruct flows.

Captured Traces: In this work we captured two traces in the live network of a mobile operator at one Gn interface. The Gn interface connects a SGSN with a GGSN. The protocol at the Gn interface is the GPRS Tunneling Protocol (GTP). This protocol allows to analyze data packets on a per user base. For details of 3G architecture, see [5].

Two traces, TR_1 and TR_2, were recorded in the last week of August and September 2008, respectively. Both traces span four hours including the busy hour in

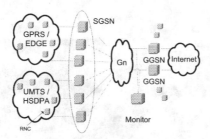

Fig. 1. Measurement Setup

the network of the operator. This allows to extract a sufficient statistic. All numbers presented are renormalized by an undisclosed value. The length of the traces was chosen in order to allow reasonable fast processing on one hand, and to offer enough input data on the other hand.

3   Detection Method

Our detection method is based on some assumptions closely related to 3G core networks. The start of a data transfer in UMTS is similar to dial-up session. The user initiates a so called Packet Data Protocol (PDP)-context, which enables him to transfer data on the IP layer. The measurement software is tracking such PDP-context creations. Therefore, we are able to identify the start of a data session, which itself addresses a unique MS by the related mobile host.

The network under test offers dynamically allocated public IP addresses for each active PDP-context. In this work the term "local" always refers to the parameters of the 3G mobile device, e.g., the public IP address. In such a case, where no network address translation takes place, Skype is mainly communicating via UDP. We focus here on the detection in such a scenario. Functionally the setting is similar with dial-up connections when, e.g., PPP protocol is used to authenticate and assign a dynamic IP address.

Structure of Skype Packets: A typical Skype packet is depicted in Fig. 2(a) [7, 8]. The first two byte of the packet represent the ID of the packet. The ID for each packet is chosen randomly. It defines a packet in a unique way, e.g., allowing retransmission requests. The next byte indicates the type of the packet, this can be interpreted as a signaling setting. There are random bits added to this byte in order to obfuscate the detection. The real function is obtained by applying a bit mask 0x1F to the byte. Table 1 gives the known byte values (Fall 2008). The rest of the packet is encrypted Skype payload.

Detecting Skype Flows: In older versions of Skype the first packet a client did send had some special properties. Following [8] the public IP address parameter in the ciphering is set to *0.0.0.0*. Note that according to [8] the public IP address of the sender is part of the encryption function. Therefore, the receiver, which

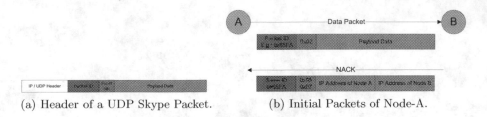

(a) Header of a UDP Skype Packet.   (b) Initial Packets of Node-A.

Fig. 2. Packet Structure of Skype Messages

Table 1. Description of the Values of the Signaling Byte

Function	Value	Description
Enc	0x02	Initial packet for encoding
NACK	0x05 or 0x07	Packet of given ID could not be decoded
Resend	0x03	Retransmitted packet
Data	0x0D	Normal data packet

used IP address stored in the IP-header, was not able to decode the arriving packet in a proper way and triggered a NACK packet. The UPD payload of this packet contains the public IP address of the client in plain text. This message identifies network address translations by the Skype software. This procedure is depicted in Fig. 2(b).

In the current version (3.1.0) the algorithm of Skype has improved compared to older versions, see [8]. After the startup the client encrypts the packets based on its last known public IP address. Therefore, in an scenario with static IP addresses the NACK message will only occur once after the software installation. However, in our network, for each PDP-context creation, a user is assigned a new IP address out of the address pool of the operator. Moreover, in our measurement period we did not observe IP re-usage for an individual user. Earlier measurements did show similar results [9]. This behavior facilitates the detection procedure.

We start tracking at the beginning of a PDP-context. Therefore, we monitor those two login packets. The detection algorithm executes for each UDP packet the following (simplified) steps:

1. *Check if the third payload byte matches any Skype function.*
   - Yes: go to **2**
   - No: go to **4**
2. *Check local UDP port with the database.*
     The database contains the IP address and port of every detected Skype user.
   - Hit: Flow is marked as Skype traffic, go to **3**
   - Otherwise: go to **3**
3. *Check if the packet is a NACK messages.*
     This is the case if and only if the UDP payload matches the follwing:

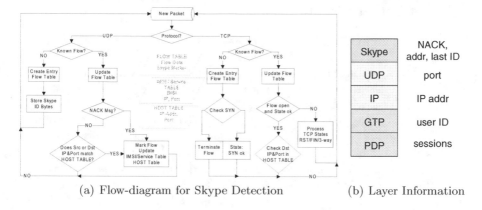

(a) Flow-diagram for Skype Detection   (b) Layer Information

Fig. 3. Principles of the Cross Layer Based Skype Detector

- The first two byte (ID) match with last seen ID to this destination.
- The third byte (function) matches to 0x05 or 0x07.
- The Skype payload length is 12 byte.
- The Skype payload contains the client IP address in plain text (4 byte).
  If the packet contains a NACK message we store the following information:
- Local user and port as active Skype client, Skype port respectively
- Remote address and port as active Skype client, Skype port respectively
4. *Wait for the next UDP packet.*

Based on these steps the method is able to mark Skype related flows. The method matches 7 byte of information in the actual packet of which 4 byte are cross-layer information (the IP address of the client) and two bytes from the previous packet (ID). The flow-diagram of the method is depicted in Fig. 3(a). Regarding the fact that one NACK packet reveals two Skype nodes it is not mandatory to catch all login packets of each client. The method will work fine as soon as the database is populated with so-called super-nodes.

The authentication process is achieved via a TCP connection, see [7]. We detect this via pattern matching like proposed in [7]. Further detection of the TCP flows is possible using the method presented in [7]. Based on the lookup table for active Skype nodes, we are also able to mark possible Skype related TCP flows, note these flows use the port related to "Skype" too. With this information we can already classify most of the TCP flows. Without the user related signaling information present in the mobile network it is hard to detect the shut down of a Skype node see [10]. In our case, we can rely on information from the lower layers, namely 3G signaling, and assume that the Skype software is active from the first monitored login packets until the termination of the PDP-context or until a packet with a non-matching third byte (function of Skype) arrives at the client. Figure 3(b) depicts the different layers we exploit and the information we gain at each layer.

Based on the fact that we exploit data on different layers to classify Skype flows we called the method "Cross Layer Based Skype Detection" (CLBSD).

4   Measurement Results

The results of this section are derived from three traces, one test trace and two live traces, TR_1 and TR_2. In the test trace two Skype nodes, both connected via the radio access network of the operator generated a VoIP call and a file transfer. In this setup the ground truth is known as both terminals did only offer the Skype service.

Our method reached a detection performance of 97.1 % with respect to volume in byte and 95.2 % in terms of packets. Analyzing the non-classified flows did show that more than 95% of the remaining flows were due to port scans and P2P "background traffic". The other flows had a destination port equal to 80 or 443. Traffic on these two ports is not classified as Skype traffic at the moment as the mis-classification rate on these ports was too high. As a solution to this problem we propose a *white list* of known servers, e.g., Google, news pages and so on, traffic of which is excluded in advance.

In the next step we analyzed TR_1 and TR_2 with our method and compared the results with TSTAT v 1.72b[1] [11]. Both traces were taken on a Tuesday afternoon including the busy hour around 8 p.m., following [12]. As the traffic is recorded on a packet level we had to create flows or connections. Regarding the term "connection", in case of TCP traffic it will refer to the plain TCP connection, for UDP traffic we define a connection as the union of all packets seen with the same quadruple (source / destination addresses and ports) with a maximum inter-packet spacing of ten minutes, see [12]. Based on this definition the traces contain on average more than ten million flows per hour (note that we cannot disclose more detailed numbers).

Table 2 presents the numbers of detected flows, packets and byte for all three methods. The flows in the table are accumulated over the tracing period. The values are normalized using our proposed method as reference, to 100%. The number of flows was in the order of 10^5.

Table 2. Classification of Skype Traffic

Trace	TR_1			TR_2		
Method	Flows	Byte	Packets	Flows	Byte	Packets
CLBSD	100%	100%	100%	100%	100%	100%
TSTAT v1.72b	89%	93%	91%	93%	94%	89%

The performance of TSTAT is slightly lower compared to our solution. As we are not allowed to store payload in any way, we are not able to post analyze the differences on the packet level. However, an investigation of the flow table of classified Skype traffic showed that the TSTAT method had problems detecting some long flows. From the duration, average packet size and data-rate of the flows, often larger than 10 minutes, we hypothesize that these flows are undetected voice or video calls. We assume that the statistical method of the used

---

[1] http://tstat.polito.it/download/tstat.v172beta.tgz

version has problems to cope with the silence suppression implemented into the new versions of Skype.

In order to get a better understanding we generated an artificial test trace between two mobile terminals. We then initiated a voice call between the two nodes. The test call included longer periods of silence on both terminals. In this setup TSTAT did not detect a voice call, while our method was able to detect this traffic based on the port mapping.

5 Summary and Conclusions

In this paper, we present a new method to detect Skype traffic flows and users tailored for a 3G network with dynamic IP addresses allocation.[2] Traces from a Gn interface of a 3G network allow a unique mapping between data packets and users. This feature allows to track Skype users in an efficient manner.

In contrast to existing methods, we do not make use of the statistical properties of the traffic flows, but rather focus on the cross-layer information within signaling of Skype. We exploit the fact that at the startup a pair of special packets is generated. If the node has received a new IP address since the last startup of the program, which is the case in most 3G networks, we are able to detect these messages. From this first flow we gain the knowledge about the presence of a Skype node, and the port it is listening on. Note that Skype uses persistently the same port under normal conditions. In the following all flows that originate or terminate at this node and port are accounted as Skype traffic. In addition to this, the TCP authentication message is traced via a pattern matching.

The advantage of the new method is the fact that a flow can be classified already when the first packet arrives. Therefore, this approach can be directly used for quality of service settings at a low cost. However, the proposed method relies totally on the detection of special signaling events that, on one hand, may change at some point in time, and on the other hand, need a change of the client IP address as a trigger. The former constraint is the same for all Skype detection methods.

The detection performance of this method is comparable to an publicly available tool, TSTAT, but offers a higher performance in terms of accuracy and computational burden. Note that we consider the low scores for TSTAT in the table to be a part of a change of the Skype codec, rather than a restrictive design of the detector. We only mark flows based on a match of 7 byte of which 4 byte are containing dynamic cross-layer information, e.g., the local IP address of the client. This is a much stronger restriction than what is found in commercial firewalls and other publications [2–4]. We believe that the mis-classification rate of our method is close to zero.

In our further work we want to change the method accordingly for networks not offering public IP addresses.

---

[2] Note, in fact this method could be used in any network which offers a dynamic allocation of public IP addresses, e.g., ADSL access networks, if the relation between customer and IP address is known, e.g., by sniffing Radius messages.

Acknowledgments

This work was part of the DARWIN+ project at the ftw. This project is supported by the COMET (Competence Centers for Excellent Technologies) initiative of the city of Vienna and hosted at the ftw in Vienna. The views expressed in this paper are those of the authors and do not necessarily reflect the views within the partners of the project.

References

[1] Ricciato, F., Svoboda, P., Hasenleithner, E., Fleischer, W.: On the Impact of Unwanted Traffic onto a 3G Network. In: Proc. of the SECPERU 2006, vol. 36(4), pp. 49–56 (2006)

[2] Kuan-Ta, C., Chun-Ying, H., Polly, H., Chin-Laung, L.: Quantifying Skype user satisfaction. In: Proc. of the SIGCOMM 2006, vol. 36(4), pp. 399–410 (2006)

[3] Bonfiglio, D., Mellia, M., Meo, M., Rossi, D., Tofanelli, P.: Revealing Skype traffic: when Randomness plays with you. In: Proc. of the SIGCOMM 2007, vol. 37(4), pp. 37–48 (2007)

[4] Bonfiglio, D., Mellia, M., Meo, M., Ritacca, N., Rossi, D.: Tracking down Skype traffic. In: Proc. of Infocom 2008, p. 5 (2008)

[5] Holma, H., Toskala, A.: WCDMA for UMTS, Radio Access For Third Generation Mobile Communications, 3rd edn. Wiley, Chichester (2004)

[6] Ricciato, F., Svoboda, P., Motz, J., Fleischer, W.: Traffic monitoring and analysis in 3g networks: lessons learned from the METAWIN project. e&i Elektrotechnik und Informationstechnik 123(7-8), 22–28 (2006)

[7] Baset, S.A., Schulzrinne, H.G.: An analysis of the skype peer-to-peer internet telephony protocol. In: Proc. of 25th IEEE ICC, April 2006, vol. 1, pp. 1–11 (2006)

[8] Biondi, P., Desclaux, F.: Silver needle in the skype. In: Proc. of Black Hat Europe 2006, vol. 1, p. 25 (2006)

[9] Ricciato, F., Vacirca, F., Svoboda, P.: Diagnosis of Capacity Bottlenecks via Passive Monitoring in 3G Networks: an Empirical Analysis. Computer Networks 57, 1205–1231 (2007)

[10] Rossi, D., Valenti, S., Veglia, P., Bonfiglio, D., Mellia, M., Meo, M.: Pictures from the skype. In: Proc. of ACM SIGMETRICS Demo Competition, vol. 1, p. 7 (2008)

[11] Mellia, M., Carpani, A., Lo Cigno, R.: Measuring IP and TCP behavior on edge nodes. In: Proc. of Globecom 2002, vol. 1, p. 5 (2002)

[12] Svoboda, P., Ricciato, F.: Composition of GPRS and UMTS traffic: snapshots from a live network. In: Proc. of the IPS MoMe 2006, vol. 4, pp. 42–54 (2006)

Incentives for BGP Guided IP-Level Topology Discovery

Benoit Donnet*

Université catholique de Louvain, CSE Deparment, Belgium

Abstract. Internet topology discovery has been an attractive research field during the past decade. In particular, the research community was interested in modeling the network as well as providing efficient tools, mostly based on traceroute, for collecting data. In this paper, we follow this track of rendering traceroute-based exploration more efficient. We discuss incentives for coupling passive monitoring and active measurements. In particular, we show that high-level information, such as BGP updates, might be used to trigger targeted traceroutes. As a result, the network dynamics might be better capture. We also provide a freely available tool for listening to BGP feeds and triggering dedicated traceroutes.

1 Introduction

The past ten years have seen a growing body of important research work on the topology of the Internet [1]. Since Faloutsos et al. seminal paper on the power-law relationships in the Internet [2], researchers strongly investigated the Internet topology at the IP, router, and AS level. The IP level considers routers and end-systems IP interfaces. The basic idea for collecting data is to probe the Internet from multiple vantage points using the technique of *traceroute*. The router level considers each router as being a single node in the topology. This is done by aggregating a router IP interfaces under a single identifier using *alias resolution*. Finally, the AS level provides information about autonomous systems (ASes) connectivity. The past research efforts were done on Internet modeling and techniques for efficiently collecting data. In this paper, we push further techniques for gathering data for the IP level Internet topology by providing incentives for using high-level information for triggering traceroute-like exploration.

The traceroute-based exploration works as follows: probes, basically UDP packets, are sent with increasing TTL values. When the TTL expires, an intermediate router is supposed to reply with an ICMP 'Time Exceeded" message to the sender. By looking at the IP source address of this ICMP message, the measurement point can learn one of the IP address of the router. When the probe

* This work has been partially supported by the European Commission-funded 034819 OneLab project. Benoit Donnet is funded by the Fonds National de la Recherche Scientifique (FNRS – Rue d'Egmont 5, 1000 Brussels).

M. Papadopouli, P. Owezarski, and A. Pras (Eds.): TMA 2009, LNCS 5537, pp. 101–108, 2009.

reaches the destination, the destination is supposed to reply with an ICMP "Destination Unreachable" message with code "port unreachable". This works if the specified port in the UDP probe is presumably unused. Extensions to traceroute have been proposed to use ICMP and TCP probes.

Unfortunately, probing this way from multiple vantage points towards a large set of destinations is somewhat inefficient. First some routers along the path are repeatedly discovered for each traceroute [3]. Second, it is time consuming. For instance, the recent *Archipelago* [4] infrastructure takes roughly three days to complete its destination list. In such a context, it is very difficult to capture the network dynamics. Efforts have been made for rendering traceroute exploration less redundant [3,5,6], allowing also to speed up the exploration process. However, this does not entirely solve the network dynamic capture issue.

In this paper, we follow this track of rendering traceroute-based exploration more efficient. As recently mentioned by Eriksson et al. "passive measurements of packet traffic offer the possibility of a greatly expanded perspective of Internet structure with much lower impact and management overhead" [7]. We echo this call by proposing a way to discover the Internet topology at the IP level by using passively collected information for triggering (and guiding) traceroute.

We propose to consider BGP information to guide probing and trigger specific targeted traceroute. In particular, we focus on updates that modify two given BGP attributes: the AS_PATH and the communities. We argue that a change in one of these attributes might be a route change indication and, thus, be considered as a trigger event for launching a traceroute towards a specific prefix. By acting so, a traceroute system might better capture network dynamics information. This is thus complementary to existing tools. In addition to this, we provide a tool for listening to BGP feed and deciding whether a traceroute must be launched or not.[1]

The remainder of this paper is organized as follows: Sec. 2 explains how BGP information might be used for guided probing; Sec. 3 discusses our implementation; Sec. 4 positions our work regarding the state of the art; finally, Sec. 5 concludes this paper by summarizing its main contributions and discussing further research directions.

2   BGP as Trigger Event

In this section, we study how some BGP events might be used to trigger targeted traceroutes. We base our evaluation on Routeviews [8] data, starting from October 1st, 2007 to September 30th, 2008. The Routeviews project aims at frequently collecting BGP table dumps and BGP update messages from the perspective of several locations. For our study, we considered three BGP routers: Dixie (Japan), Equinix (United States of America), and Isc (United States of America). Finally, we only took into account IPv4 routes.

---

[1] The code is freely available, under a BSD-like license at `http://gforge.info.ucl.ac.be/projects/bgpprobing/`

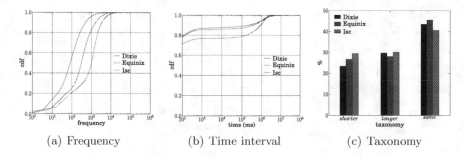

(a) Frequency   (b) Time interval   (c) Taxonomy

Fig. 1. AS_PATH modification

2.1   AS_PATH

The AS_PATH is a standard BGP attribute that is used to list the ASes a route advertisement has traversed. For a given prefix, if the AS_PATH is modified between two BGP updates or between a BGP update and the current record in the routing table, it means that the path has changed. This can be seen as a trigger event for a traceroute exploration towards the source prefix advertised in the BGP update.

Fig. 1 shows statistics on the AS_PATH modification over time. In particular, Fig. 1(a) shows the cumulative distribution of modifications frequency (horizontal axis in log-scale), i.e., how many times, for each prefix, the AS_PATH has changed over the considered period. Fig. 1(b) shows the time interval (in ms – horizontal axis in log-scale) between two AS_PATH modifications for a given prefix.

We see that in 50% of the cases, an AS_PATH is modified more than 1000 times for the Isc router (Fig. 1(a)). However, the time interval between two modifications is extremely short (less than 100ms) in 80% of the case (Fig. 1(b)), probably due to a path exploration process. Nevertheless, there is a kind of plateau between 1.000 and 1.000.000ms in the remaining 20%, suggesting so that AS_PATH changes might be somewhat "persistent".

Fig 1(c) gives, for each Routeviews router, the taxonomy of the BGP AS_PATH attribute modification. An AS_PATH can be *shorter* (the new AS_PATH counts less intermediate ASes than the recorded one), *longer* (the new AS_PATH counts more intermediate ASes than the recorded one), or *same length* (the new AS_PATH counts the same number of ASes than the recorded one but at least, one of them is different). It is interesting to notice that, in most of the cases, the modified AS_PATH has the same length that the previous AS_PATH.

2.2   BGP Communities

The BGP communities attribute provides a way of grouping destinations into a single entity, named *community*, to which similar routing decisions might be

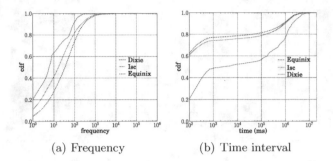

(a) Frequency   (b) Time interval

Fig. 2. BGP communities attribute modification

applied. A BGP communities attribute is composed of one or more 32 bits numbers. These numbers are structured as follows: the high-order 16 bits represent an AS number, while the low-order 16 bits define the semantic of the value. Each AS can use the 2^{16} communities whose high-order 16 bits are equal to its own AS number.

Donnet and Bonaventure recently showed that the BGP communities attribute is more and more used [9]. They further proposed a classification of BGP communities usage. They identified three classes:

- *inbound* communities refer to communities added or used when a route is received by a router on an eBGP session. It is typically used for setting a particular value to the LOCAL_PREF attribute (i.e., the degree of preference for an external route) or for tagging route with the location where it was received from an external peer.
- *outbound* communities are used by a router to filter BGP announcements for traffic engineering purposes. A community is inserted by the originator of the route in order to influence its redistribution by downstream routers.
- *blackhole* communities refers to a particular BGP community used by an ISP to block packets. These communities are used only inside ISPs and should not be distributed on the global Internet.

It is clear that a change in inbound communities (in particular those tagging the received route) might indicate a change in the path a packet follows and, thus, be considered as traceroute trigger-event.

In the fashion of Fig. 1, Fig. 2 presents statistics on the BGP communities attribute modification. We see that modifications are much less frequent than for the AS_PATH attribute, while we observe the same kind of behavior for the time interval between changes.

In the fashion of the AS_PATH, the time interval between two BGP communities attribute modification is quite short. Except for Dixie, in 60% of the cases, the time interval is less or equal to 100ms.

Up to now, we have seen that BGP communities might change over time. If we are able to identify to which class (see Donnet and Bonaventure for details [9])

Table 1. Classification of BGP communities changes

Router	Inbound				Outbound	
	IXP	Type of Peer	Geographic	AS	Announcement	prepending
Dixie	0.27%	7.14%	1.01%	1.33%	4.96%	0.11%
Equinix	16.75%	52.52%	30.01%	0%	0.93%	0.51%
Isc	0.06%	20.78%	43.55%	0.08%	2.88%	0.59%

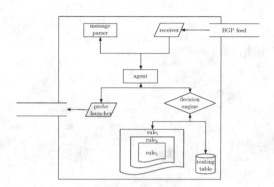

Fig. 3. Interactions between modules

belong the modified communities attribute, we can potentially trigger traceroute. Using the database provided by Donnet and Bonaventure, we tried to perform this classification on our six months dataset. Results are shown in Table 1. It provides a proportion of modified BGP communities we were able to classified. Due to the lack of standardization and documentation of the BGP communities attribute, we were not able to classify all the BGP communities (in particular for Dixie). We however identified an interesting proportion of modifications in "Geographic" BGP communities attribute (for instance, 43.55% for Isc). This means that, for the Isc router, in 43.55% of the cases, a modification of the BGP communities attribute concerns the geographic location of a route received from an external peer.

Such an observation is of keen interest of us as it clearly indicates a route change and is thus a good trigger-event for a traceroute exploration.

3   Implementation

We implemented a tool for listening to BGP updates and determine whether a traceroute must be triggered or not towards a particular prefix. Fig. 3 shows a high-level view of our implementation.

The *Receiver* module aims at listening to BGP incoming BGP messages. These BGP messages can directly come from a BGP feed provided by local operator (byte streams as defined in RFC 1771 [10]) or from the BGPMon project [11] (XML files as defined by Cheng et al. [12] - a particular message parser then be implemented). The *Decision* module is in charge of deciding whether the received message can trigger a traceroute or not. This decision is based on existing information (the routing table - the system uses an existing routing table as input and this routing table is updated with incoming messages) and the applications of *rules*. Currently, four rules have been implemented:

- Withdraw rule. An existing route is suppressed from the routing table.
- Add rule. A non-existing route is added to the routing table.
- AS_PATH rule. The AS_PATH attribute of an existing route changes (as discussed in Sec. 2.1).
- BGP communities rule. The BGP communities attribute of an existing route changes (as explained in Sec. 2.2).

The system has been implemented so that a new rule can be easily implemented and added to the system.

Nevertheless, even if one of the rules above is matched, it does not necessarily trigger a traceroute. Several conditions must be checked before. Indeed, some prefixes might generate route flapping [14] or be in a path exploration process. In such a case, traceroute should not be launched. A traceroute will be triggered at the following conditions:

- The prefix contained in the message did not trigger a traceroute recently. A timed-cache (i.e., a timer is associated to each entry in the cache), system has been implemented to avoid to constantly probing the same prefix. If the prefix is in the cache, the traceroute is not trigger and the associated timer in the cache is reset. At the timer expiration, the corresponding entry is removed from the cache.
- The received BGP message is not considered as noise. A received prefix is considered as noise if it belongs to the top 20 of unstable prefix (according to Geof Huston weekly report [13]) or if the route is flapping (route flap damping algorithms have been implemented [14,15]).
- The token bucket is not full. In order to avoid flooding the traceroute server and the network, traceroute are triggered at a certain rate.

4   Related Work

Systems, such as RIPE NCC *TTM* [16] and NLANR *AMP* [17], consider a larger set of monitor, several hundreds, but avoid to trace outside their own network. A more recent tool, *DIMES* [18], is publicly released as a daemon. *Rocketfuel* [5] focuses on the topology of a given ISP and not on the whole Internet topology as skitter does, for instance. *Scriptroute* [6] is a system that allows an ordinary Internet user to perform network measurements from several distributed vantage points. Finally, the recent *iPlane* constructs an annotated map of the Internet and evaluates end-to-end performances (latency, bandwidth, capacity, etc). Finally, the recently deployed *Archipelago* [4] probes all routed /24 from several locations. Others have proposed improvements to traceroute for reducing measurement redundancy [3,19] or for avoiding anomalies [20]. None of these aforementioned works provide a link with higher level information, such as BGP, to guide probing.

Finally, topology discovery might be done through a deployment facility. Examples of such a system are *m-coop* [21], *pMeasure* [22], and *DipZoom* [23]. These solutions are complementary to our tool as they can be used to dispatch the traceroute trigger to several vantage points.

5 Conclusion

The Internet topology at the IP interface level has attracted the attention of the research community for a long time now. People are interested in modeling the network as well as in traceroute-based tools for efficiently collecting data.

In this paper, we made a step towards a more network-friendly traceroute-based system. Indeed, we discussed incentives for considering high-level information, such as BGP data, as a trigger event for targeted traceroutes. In particular, we focused on two BGP attributes, the AS_PATH and the communities. We believe that a tracing system using this kind of information can increase its coverage capabilities by better capturing network dynamics. In addition, we provide a freely available implementation of a tool for listening to BGP feed and deciding whether a traceroute must be sent or not.

A deployment of our tool using for instance BGPMon [11] should reveal, in the near future, to what extend we are able to capture network dynamics.

References

1. Donnet, B., Friedman, T.: Internet topology discovery: a survey. IEEE Communications Surveys and Tutorials 9(4), 2–15 (2007)
2. Faloutsos, M., Faloutsos, P., Faloutsos, C.: On power-law relationships of the internet topology. In: Proc. ACM SIGCOMM (September 1999)
3. Donnet, B., Raoult, P., Friedman, T., Crovella, M.: Efficient algorithms for large-scale topology discovery. In: Proc. ACM SIGMETRICS (June 2005)
4. claffy, k., Hyun, Y., Keys, K., Fomenkov, M.: Internet mapping: from art to science. In: Proc. IEEE Cybersecurity Applications and Technologies Conference for Homeland Security (CATCH) (March 2009)
5. Spring, N., Mahajan, R., Wetherall, D.: Measuring ISP topologies with Rocketfuel. In: Proc. ACM SIGCOMM (August 2002)
6. Spring, N., Wetherall, D., Anderson, T.: Scriptroute: A public internet measurement facility. In: Proc. USENIX Symposium on Internet Technologies and Systems (USITS) (March 2002)
7. Eriksson, B., Barford, P., Nowak, R.: Network discovery from passive measurements. In: Proc. ACM SIGCOMM (August 2008)
8. University of Oregon: Route views, University of Oregon Route Views project See, http://www.routeviews.org/
9. Donnet, B., Bonaventure, O.: On BGP communities. ACM SIGCOMM Computer Communication Review 38(2), 55–59 (2008)
10. Rekhter, Y., Watson, T.J.: A border gateway protocol 4 (BGP-4). RFC 1771, Internet Engineering Task Force (March 1995)

11. Yan, H., Matthews, D., Burnett, K., Massey, D., Oliveira, R., Zhang, L.: BGP-mon: a real-time, scalable, extensible monitoring system. In: Proc. IEEE Cyberse-curity Applications and Technologies Conference for Homeland Security (CATCH) (March 2009)
12. Cheng, P., Yan, H., Brunett, K., Massey, D., Zhang, L.: BGP routing information in XML format. Internet Draft (Work in Progress) draft-cheng-grow-bgp-xml-00, Internet Engineering Task Force (February 2009)
13. Huston, G.: BGP update report (2008), See: http://www.potaroo.net
14. Villamizar, C., Chandra, R., Govindan, R.: BGP route flap damping. RFC 2439, Internet Engineering Task Force (November 1998)
15. Mao, Z.M., Govindan, R., Varghese, G., Katz, R.H.: Route flap damping exacer-bates internet routing convergence. In: Proc. ACM SIGCOMM (August 2002)
16. Georgatos, F., Gruber, F., Karrenberg, D., Santcroos, M., Susanj, A., Uijterwaal, H., Wilhelm, R.: Providing active measurements as a regular service for ISPs. In: Proc. Passive and Active Measurement Workshop (PAM) (April 2001)
17. McGregor, A., Braun, H.W., Brown, J.: The NLANR network analysis infrastruc-ture. IEEE Communications Magazine 38(5) (2000)
18. Shavitt, Y., Shir, E.: DIMES: Let the internet measure itself. ACM SIGCOMM Computer Communication Review 35(5) (October 2005)
19. Donnet, B., Friedman, T., Crovella, M.: Improved algorithms for network topology discovery. In: Dovrolis, C. (ed.) PAM 2005. LNCS, vol. 3431, pp. 149–162. Springer, Heidelberg (2005)
20. Augustin, B., Cuvellier, X., Orgogozo, B., Viger, F., Friedman, T., Latapy, M., Magnien, C., Teixeira, R.: Avoiding anomalies with paris traceroute. In: Proc. ACM USENIX Internet Measurement Conference (IMC) (October 2006)
21. Srinivasan, S., Zegura, E.W.: Network measurement as a cooperative enterprise. In: Druschel, P., Kaashoek, M.F., Rowstron, A. (eds.) IPTPS 2002. LNCS, vol. 2429, pp. 166–177. Springer, Heidelberg (2002)
22. Liu, W., Boutaba, R., Won-Ki Hong, J.: pMeasure: a tool for measuring the inter-net. In: Proc. 2nd Workshop on End-to-End Monitoring Techniques and Services (E2EMON) (October 2004)
23. Wen, Z., Triukose, S., Rabinovich, M.: Facilitatiing focused Internet measurements. In: Proc. ACM SIGMETRICS (June 2007)

Scaling Analysis of Wavelet Quantiles in Network Traffic

Giada Giorgi and Claudio Narduzzi

University of Padova, Dept. of Information Engineering,
via Gradenigo 6/B, I-35100 Padova, Italy

Abstract. The study of network traffic by flow analysis has been the subject of intense and varied research. Wavelet transforms, which form the core of most traffic analysis tools, are known to be robust to linear trends in data measurements, but may suffer from the presence of occasional non-stationarities.

This paper considers how the information associated to quantiles of wavelet coefficients can be exploited to improve the understanding of traffic features. A tool based on these principles is introduced and results of its application to analysis of traffic traces are presented.

1 Introduction

Statistical traffic analysis refers to the general properties of network traffic, aiming to describe them by suitable flow models. Traffic in packet networks has been the subject of intense and varied research, leading to progressive refinements of models and analysis tools.

When the statistical features of flow intensity in a traffic trace are analyzed, it can be seen that anomalies, associated to local changes in the distribution of traffic, frequently affect the tails of the empirical probability density function (pdf). Effects of a similar nature may also arise when a highly composite traffic trace is considered, in which case distribution changes may be attributed to the varying mix of contributions from flows having different statistical properties. These issues are directly related to the assumed traffic model: in a number of cases of practical interest, forcing a single-flow LRD random process model on measured data does not appear to suit the actual situation entirely [1], [2].

The well-known *Abry-Veitch* (A-V) wavelet-based tool has become a standard reference for most traffic analysis methods [3]. However, analysis of real traffic traces showed that, in the cases mentioned above, the tool may not provide meaningful measurements of the Hurst scaling exponent [4] and of other parameters. A reason why the A-V tool is not ideally suited to deal with these kinds of phenomena, is that it refers to a cumulative quantity, i.e., the energy of wavelet coefficients. From a statistical viewpoint this emphasises variance, which is sensitive to changes in empirical pdf's but does not allow a more detailed understanding of phenomena.

This paper will show that quantile analysis of wavelet coefficients, on the contrary, can provide very robust and acceptably accurate estimates of the Hurst

M. Papadopouli, P. Owezarski, and A. Pras (Eds.): TMA 2009, LNCS 5537, pp. 109–116, 2009.

parameter value, even in the presence of non-stationary disturbances in traffic time series. The probability level of quantiles represents an additional parameter, that can be tuned for the purposes of the analysis. Comparison between curves obtained for different confidence levels may provide additional information on the features of the analysed traffic.

2   Scaling and Wavelets

The proposed approach merges concepts from quantile analysis with the wavelet multiresolution approach, whose main features are briefly recalled in this Section.

Let $X(k)$ be a time series obtained by counting the number of packets (or bytes) flowing through a link during consecutive, non-overlapping time slots of duration T. Packet counts can be aggregated over larger time scales. Considering time intervals of progressively longer duration $2^j \cdot T$, the time series:

$$X^{(j)}(k) = \frac{1}{2^j} \sum_{i=0}^{2^j-1} X(k \cdot 2^j + i) \tag{1}$$

represents the aggregate version of the time series $X(k)$ at scale j. Under the hypothesis of self-similarity for $X(k)$, the following relationship can be found:

$$X^{(j)}(k) \stackrel{d}{=} 2^{j(H-1)} X(k), \tag{2}$$

where $\stackrel{d}{=}$ denotes equality of probability distributions and H is the Hurst exponent. It is well known, e.g., from the early pioneering studies presented in [5], that the correlation structure of the time series $X(k)$ can be assumed to decrease with a power law as the lag number increases. This statistical property is called *long-range dependence* (LRD). The Hurst parameter H quantifies the asymptotic self-similar scaling as well as the degree of long-range dependence. Under the common assumption that the underlying random process is fractional with stationary increments, H varies between 0.5 and 1, denoting respectively a non-correlated and a completely correlated time series.

For a self-similar process a scaling relationship among wavelet coefficients exists [6] and has the same form for both approximation coefficients $a_x(j,k)$ and detail coefficients $d_x(j,k)$. Using the symbol $c_x(j,k)$ to generically indicate either of the two set of coefficients, it can be given in the form:

$$c_x(j,k) \stackrel{d}{=} 2^{j(H+\frac{1}{2})} c_x(0,k), \tag{3}$$

where $\stackrel{d}{=}$ denotes equality of probability distributions. It should be remembered that, if the definition of aggregate process given in (1) is referred to, the relationship must be normalized by the number of samples considered in the summation, yielding:

$$c_x(j,k) \stackrel{d}{=} 2^{j(H-\frac{1}{2})} c_x(0,k). \tag{4}$$

Recursive algorithms are initialized with $c_x(0,k) = X(k)$.

The *Abry-Veitch* estimator considers the energy of detail coefficients $d_x(j, k)$ at different time scales. This follows the scaling law:

$$\mathbb{E}\left[d_x(j,k)^2\right] = 2^{j(2H-1)}\mathbb{E}\left[d_x(0,k)^2\right],\tag{5}$$

which provides a means to identify the presence of long range dependence in data measurements and estimate the corresponding scaling exponent H. It can be noted that, since the mean of detail coefficients is zero: $\mathbb{E}\left[d_x(j,k)\right] = 0$, the energy (5) corresponds to the coefficient variance.

The tool has been largely used to identify the presence of scaling in data measurements and to estimate the value of the scaling exponent by a linear regression on the log-log wavelet spectrum diagram. Since the detail coefficients are uncorrelated, its variance is a function of the amount of data considered and does not depend on the unknown, actual value of the Hurst coefficient H. This very important property allows to improve estimation accuracy by increasing the number of samples and is one of the reasons for the success of the tool.

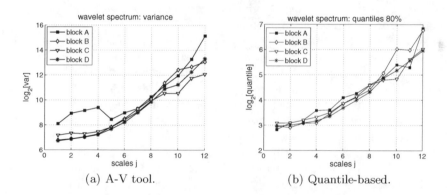

(a) A-V tool.   (b) Quantile-based.

Fig. 1. Wavelet spectrum over consecutive non-overlapping blocks

3   A-V Analysis of a Non-stationary Trace

The A-V estimator is known to be robust to linear trends in data measurements, but may suffer from the presence of occasional non-stationarities. An example is provided by the following analysis of the AUCK [7] traffic trace captured on 06 April 2001, which presents a strong, localised non-stationarity. The raw traffic trace was initially aggregated over time intervals of duration $T = 50\ ms$. Analysis is restricted to measurements taken during the day working hours, by considering only the samples between the $(6.5E + 05)$-th and the $(11.5E + 05)$-th. This allows to disregard longer-term fluctuations of traffic on a daily scale. The discrete wavelet transform was applied over four non-overlapping blocks of $125,000$ samples each (roughly a two-hour lenght); the wavelet spectra obtained in each block are plotted together in Fig. 1(a). It can be seen that, at lower time

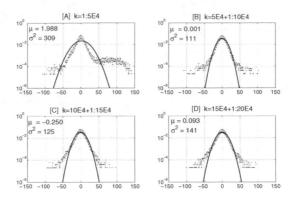

Fig. 2. Histograms of the wavelet detail coefficient $d_x(j, k)$ calculated over consecutive non-overlapping blocks. The analysis refers to the AUCKIV trace of the 06 April 2001.

scales, the curve related to *block A*, which entirely contains the non-stationarity, presents a strong discrepancy from the others.

Recall that the Hurst parameter characterizes the dependence of the traffic only a large scales. However the wavelet spectrum provides additional useful information about the dependence in the data also on small time scales. In this case, where an alignment can be found at the lowest scales [3], that is from $j_1 = 1$ to an upper bound j_2, the scaling indicates the fractal nature of the traffic.

To understand the influence of this local flow irregularity on wavelet spectra, the time series of the lowest-scale detail coefficients $d_x(1, k)$ have been considered for the same four blocks. Their histograms are presented in Fig. 2, where they are compared with Gaussian distributions having the same mean and variance. *Block A* is characterised by an asymmetric histogram with a much heavier tail for positive values of detail coefficients; the estimated variance is accordingly larger than in the other blocks.

As can be noted in Fig. 1(a), the non-stationarity affects the time series over time scales in the range between $j_1 = 1$ and $j_2 = 4$. The wavelet spectrum obtained by the A-V tool represents, over these scales, the behaviour of the non-stationarity and not that of the main process.

Similar effects are known and have been noted in a number of works, e.g., [8]. The consequences are that scaling analysis becomes harder, since alignments in a log energy-scale diagram are more difficult to find.

The analysis of quantiles provides additional information about the distribution of detail coefficients. Estimated quantile values for the four blocks of the AUCK traffic trace show that the local features in *block A* only affect quantiles associated with probability levels $\geq 99\%$. Lower probability levels are not affected by the presence of disturbances in the traffic time series.

It is important to investigate how this additional knowledge could be interpreted correctly. In this example, analysis of quantiles referring to a probability level $< 99\%$ could provide more accurate scaling information. On the other hand, quantiles with higher probability levels might convey information about local features.

4   Quantile-Based Estimation

Let $r_\gamma(j)$ be the $(1\text{-}\gamma)$-quantile of coefficients at scale j. It provides a bound on the value that the samples of $c_x(j,k)$ can assume, which can be exceeded with a probability γ, called *violation probability*:

$$P\left[c_x(j,k) \leq r_\gamma(j)\right] = 1 - \gamma. \tag{6}$$

The self-similarity relationship between $c_x(0,k)$ and $c_x(j,k)$ extends to their quantiles, providing the following expression that links quantiles at different scales:

$$r_\gamma(j) - \mathbb{E}[c_x(j,k)] = 2^{j\left(H-\frac{1}{2}\right)}\left[r_\gamma(0) - \mathbb{E}[c_x(j,k)]\right]. \tag{7}$$

It should be remembered that for detail coefficients, i.e., when $c_x(j,k) = d_x(j,k)$, the mean value is null. In this case the scaling relationship between quantiles can be obtained in a straightforward manner by substituting (4) in (6). It results in:

$$P\left[2^{j(H-\frac{1}{2})}d_x(0,k) \leq r_\gamma(j)\right] = P\left[d_x(0,k) \leq r_\gamma(j) \cdot 2^{-j(H-\frac{1}{2})}\right] = 1 - \gamma. \tag{8}$$

where $P\left[d_x(0,k) \leq r_\gamma(0)\right] = 1 - \gamma$ for definition. This provides the expression (7) where $\mathbb{E}[d_x(j,k)] = 0$.

Rewriting expression (7) in a log-log scale shows that the scaling exponent can be obtained by a simple process.

Graphically, a plot of log-quantile versus scale is obtained; borrowing from [8], this will be called a *quantile-based wavelet spectrum*. A linear regression of this plot then yields the scaling exponent, from which an estimate of the Hurst parameter H follows immediately.

For the AUCK trace considered in Sec. 3, the quantile-based wavelet spectra have been plotted in Fig. 1(b), with a probability level $(1-\gamma) = 80\%$. The same partitioning scheme of Fig. 1(a) has been adopted. It can be noted that the quantile-based spectrum related to *block A* is very similar to the curves obtained from the other blocks. In fact, the non-stationarity located within that block does not affect quantile estimates at the 80% level of probability. As a consequence, variability in Hurst parameter estimation is much reduced.

To gain a better understanding of the potentiality of a quantile approach, it was tested on a large amount of traffic traces. In the following we will report the results obtained for one of the traffic traces collected by the DIRT research group at the University of North Carolina (UNC). These traffic traces are particularly useful because they have been thoroughly analyzed, identifying and localizing a number of features that made correct estimation of the Hurst parameter by the A-V tool quite difficult. Therefore, we employed them to test the effectiveness of the proposed approach.

The considered trace was captured on 09 April 2002; it has been aggregated over time intervals of $T = 1ms$. It presents a burst of about $300-400$ seconds duration. This burst gives rise to a strong non-stationarity that affects the medium time scales, as can be noted from the variance-based wavelet spectrum of detail coefficients in Fig. 3(a). In this case no alignment can be found, resulting in very poor estimates for H.

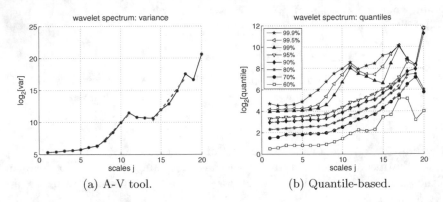

(a) A-V tool.   (b) Quantile-based.

Fig. 3. Wavelet spectrum for the UNC02 trace, captured 09 Apr. 2002 from 19:30 to 21:30

The corresponding quantile-based wavelet spectrum for the same trace is plotted in Fig. 3(b), where the curves obtained for different probability levels are shown. If probability levels $\leq 95\%$ are considered, curves are not affected by the presence of the non-stationarity, therefore alignments can be found for certain scale ranges, as illustrated by dotted lines. At those time scales the scaling exponent can be correctly estimated. Interestingly, quantile-based wavelet spectra show the same familiar two-slope behavior that generally characterizes most traffic traces.

For lower probability levels, like 60%, the quantile spectrum presents a greater variability. To explain this matter, the uncertainty associated to the estimates of quantile must be taken into account. For a random process, having a probability density function (pdf) $f(\cdot)$, the estimation variance of the theoretical $(1 - \gamma)-$quantile is:

$$\sigma^2_{r_\gamma(j)} = \frac{\gamma(1-\gamma)}{N_j \cdot f^2(r_\gamma(j))}. \tag{9}$$

where N_j is the number of samples considered for estimating the quantile.

Quantile properties therefore depend on the probability distribution of the process [9]. The uncertainty associated to quantile estimates presents a maximum for $\gamma = 50\%$ and minimum values for $\gamma = 0\%$ and $\gamma = 100\%$. For the purposes of uncertainty analysis, the distribution of measurement data can be approximated by a Gaussian process. It is important to remember the limits of this idealization. In the case of actual processes, where the tails of the distribution are generally limited by some physical constraint, the Gaussian hypothesis no longer holds for values of γ close to 0 or to 1. This discrepancy can be overcome by considering values of γ for which the Gaussian hypothesis holds true, at least as an approximation. Analysis of experimental data by normal probability plots can help find suitable limiting values [10].

This explain the greater variability at lower probability levels as well as at higher levels, as can be noted in Fig. 3(b).

5   Conclusions

The study of quantiles is better suited to deal with the heavy-tail phenomena that characterize network traffic. Its application in quantile-based wavelet spectra, that can be referred to both detail and approximation coefficients of a wavelet transform is, to the authors' knowledge, a novel idea that appears quite promising. It is important, however, to approach the method with a degree of caution.

Results shown in this paper suggest that the accuracy of Hurst parameter estimates can be improved by tuning the choice of quantile probability level. It should be realised that, in so doing, an experimenter is deliberately discarding information contained in the heavy-tails. This choice has a considerable impact in determining what is actually being modelled in a traffic flow. For instance, if traffic irregularities are related to local phenomena, the network flow could be described by a "mainstream" process, whose statistical properties may be altered by occasional outliers. If the "contamination" is not self-similar, its presence would only be evident at well-defined time scales of influence, while for larger time scales it is smoothed out by aggregation. In a similar case, information obtained by considering wavelet spectra for higher probability quantiles and by tracking their evolution with time would be just as valuable.

In general, traffic analysis can present difficulties when complex and heterogeneous flows are considered. Then, a different modelling paradigm can be considered by decomposing the flow in the monitored link into a superposition of stochastic processes, each having its own specific correlation structure. In this case analysis of wavelet quantiles would provide a more detailed picture of traffic features and might prove to be a more flexible tool.

References

1. Sarvotham, S., Riedi, R., Baraniuk, R.: Network and user driven alpha-beta on-off source model for network traffic. Computer Networks 48(3), 335–350 (2005)
2. Giorgi, G., Narduzzi, C.: A study of measurement-based traffic models for network diagnostics. In: Proc. IEEE Instrum. Meas. Tech. Conf. IMTC 2007, Warsaw, Poland, May 01-03 (2007)
3. Abry, P., Taqqu, M.S., Veitch, D.: Wavelets for the analysis, estimation and synthesis of scaling data. In: Park, K., Willinger, W. (eds.) Self Similar Traffic Analysis and Performance Evaluation. Wiley, Chichester (2000)

4. Giorgi, G., Narduzzi, C.: Rate-interval curves: A tool for the analysis and monitoring of network traffic. Performance Evaluation 65(6-7), 441–462 (2008)
5. Leland, W., Taqqu, M., Willinger, W., Wilson, D.: On the self-similar nature of ethernet traffic (extended version). IEEE/ACM Trans. on Information Theory 2(1), 1–15 (1994)
6. Pesquet-Popescu, B.: Statistical properties of the wavelet decomposition of certain non-gaussian self-similar processes. Signal Processing 75, 303–322 (1999)
7. National Laboratory for Applied Network Reasearch, U, http://mna.nlanr.net
8. Stoev, S., Taqqu, M., Marron, J.: On the wavelet spectrum diagnostic for hurst parameter estimation in the analysis of internet traffic. Computer Networks 48(3), 423–445 (2005)
9. Ivchenko, G., Medvedev, Y.: Mathematical Statistics. Mir, Moscow, Russia (1990)
10. Giorgi, G., Narduzzi, C.: Uncertainty of quantiles estimates in the measurement of self-similar processes. In: Proc. of inter. Workshop on Advanced Methods for Uncertainty Estimation in Measurement, AMUEM 2008, Sardagna, Trento, Italy, July 21-22 (2008)

KISS: Stochastic Packet Inspection*

Alessandro Finamore[1], Marco Mellia[1], Michela Meo[1], and Dario Rossi[2]

[1] Politecnico di Torino
[2] TELECOM ParisTech
lastname@tlc.polito.it, dario.rossi@enst.fr

Abstract. This paper proposes KISS, a new Internet classification method. Motivated by the expected raise of UDP traffic volume, which stems from the momentum of P2P streaming applications, we propose a novel statistical payload-based classification framework, targeted to UDP traffic.

Statistical signatures are automatically inferred from training data, by the means of a Chi-Square like test, which extracts the protocol "syntax", but ignores the protocol semantic and synchronization rules. The signatures feed a decision engine based on Support Vector Machines. KISS is tested in different scenarios, considering both data, VoIP, and traditional P2P Internet applications. Results are astonishing. The average True Positive percentage is 99.6%, with the worst case equal 98.7%. Less than 0.05% of False Positives are detected.

1   Introduction

Last years witnessed a very fast-paced evolution of new Internet applications, ignited by the introduction of the very successful P2P networking paradigm and fueled by the growth of Internet access rates. This entailed not only a deep change of the Internet application landscape, but also undermined the reliability of the traditional Internet traffic classification mechanisms, typically based on Deep Packet Inspection (DPI) such as simple port-based classification. Indeed, DPI classification is deemed to fail more and more due to proliferation of proprietary and evolving protocols and the adoption of strong encryption techniques [1,2].

In previous proposals, UDP has usually been neglected in favor of applications running over TCP. Motivated by the expected raise of UDP traffic volume, we propose a novel classification framework that explicitly targets long-lived UDP traffic.

Recalling that a protocol specifies the rules governing the *syntax*, *semantics*, and *synchronization* of a communication, we propose to extract the L7-protocol *syntax* while ignoring the actual semantic and synchronization rules. This is achieved by statistically characterizing the frequencies of observed values in the UDP payload, by performing a test similar to the Pearson's χ^2 test. The χ^2 values are then used to compactly represent application fingerprints, which we call Chi-Square Signatures - ChiSS (pronounced as in KISS). Compared to classic DPI classifiers, KISS uses statistical signatures, rather than deterministic values. This makes it more robust to protocol dialects/evolution,

---

* This work was funded by the European Commission under the 7th Framework Programme Strep Project "NAPA-WINE" (Network Aware Peer-to-Peer Application over Wise Network)

M. Papadopouli, P. Owezarski, and A. Pras (Eds.): TMA 2009, LNCS 5537, pp. 117–125, 2009.

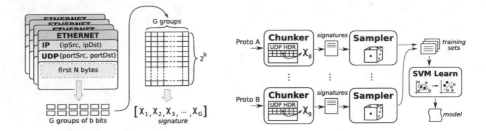

Fig. 1. Scheme of signature extraction process (left) and KISS learning steps (right)

eventual packet sampling, drop or reordering, and it does not assume to observe specific packets in a flow (e.g., the first few packets).

After the fingerprints have been extracted, proper classification must be achieved, i.e., individual items should be placed into the most likely class. A huge set of methodologies are available from the literature, that span from simple threshold based heuristics [3], to Naive Bayesian classifiers [2,4], to advanced statistical classification techniques [5]. In this paper, we rely on Support Vector Machines (SVMs) [5], which are well known in the statistical classification field, and only recently have been adopted in the context of Internet traffic classification.

2   KISS Description

2.1   Chi-Square Signatures Definition

The signature creation is inspired by the Chi-Square statistical test. The original test estimates the goodness-of-fit between observed samples of a random variable and a given theoretical distribution. Assume that the possible outcomes of an experiment are K different values and O_k are the empirical frequencies of the observed for values, out of M total observations ($\sum O_k = M$). Let E_k be the number of expected observations of k for the theoretical distribution, $E_k = M \cdot p_k$ with p_k the probability of value k. Given that M is large, the distribution of the random variable

$$X = \sum_{k=1}^{K} \frac{(O_k - E_k)^2}{E_k} \qquad (1)$$

that represents the distance between the observed empirical and theoretical distributions, can be approximated by a Chi-Square, or χ^2, distribution with $K - 1$ degrees of freedom. In the classical goodness of fit test, the values of X are compared with the typical values of a Chi-Square distributed random variable: the frequent occurrence of low probability values is interpreted as an indication of a bad fitting.

In KISS, we build a similar experiment analyzing the content of groups of bits taken from the packet payload we want to classify; we then check for the distance between the observed values and uniformly distributed bits. In other terms, we use a Chi-Square like test to measure the randomness of groups of bits as an implicit estimate of the source entropy.

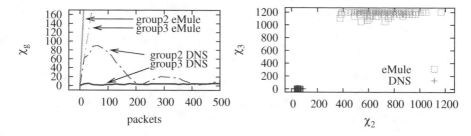

Fig. 2. Evolution in time (left) and dispersions in space (right) of χ^2 of two groups extracted from the second byte of UDP payloads

Chi-Square signatures are built from *streams* of packets directed to or originated from the same end-point. The first N bytes of the packets payload are divided into G *groups* of b consecutive bits each; a group g can take integer values in $[0, 2^b - 1]$. From packets of the same stream, we collect, for each group g, the number of observations of each value $i \in [0, 2^b - 1]$; denote it by $O_i^{(g)}$. We then define a window of C packets, in which we compute:

$$\chi_g = \sum_{i=0}^{2^b-1} \frac{\left(O_i^{(g)} - E_i\right)^2}{E_i} \quad \text{with} \quad E_i = \frac{C}{2^b} \tag{2}$$

and collect them in the KISS signature vector:

$$\overline{\chi} = [\chi_1, \chi_2, \cdots, \chi_G] \tag{3}$$

The left plot of Fig. 1 shows a schematic representation of the KISS signature extraction.

The rationale behind KISS signatures is that they allow to automatically discover application layer message header without needing to care about specific values of the header fields. Indeed, in the first bytes of UDP payload there is the application header containing fields that can be: constant identifiers, counters, words from a small dictionary (message/protocol type, flags, etc), or truly random values coming from encryption or compression algorithms. These coarse classes of fields can be easily distinguished through the operation in (2). For example, left plot in Fig. 2 reports the value of two 4-bit long groups belonging to two different traffic protocols, namely DNS and eMule, versus C. The steep lines corresponding to groups taken from an eMule stream refer to fields that are almost constant. In this case, the longer the experiment is (larger C), the larger the distance from the uniform distribution is, i.e., the bits are far from being random. In the same plot, observe the lines referring to DNS traffic. The lowest one has a very slow increase with C, its behavior is almost perfectly random, the values of χ_3 being compatible with those of a Chi-Square distribution. The bouncing line, instead, corresponds to the typical behavior of a counter. The computation (2) over consecutive groups of bits of a counter cyclically varies from very low values (when all the values have been seen the same number of times) to large values. The periodicity of this behavior depends on the group position inside the counter.

While randomness provides a coarse classification over individual groups, by jointly considering a set of G groups through the vector $\overline{\chi}$ the fingerprint becomes extremely accurate. To justify this assertion, let observe the right plot in Fig. 2, which shows signatures generated using $C = 80$ packets of a stream. Points in the figure are plotted using (χ_2, χ_3) as coordinates; each point corresponds to a different stream. Points obtained from DNS streams are displaced in the low left corner of the plot; points from eMule are spread in the top part of the plot. Intuitively, different protocols fall in different areas that are clearly identified and easily separable.

The signature creation approach previously presented is based on a number of parameters whose setting may be critical. These are the criteria we used to set them:

Bits per group ($b = 4$), whose choice trade-offs opposite needs. From one hand, b should be as closest as possible to typical length of protocol fields, e.g., b should be 4 or 8 or a multiple of 8. From the other hand, b should be small enough to allow that the packet window C over which the Chi-Square test is statistically significant is not too large, so that streams can be classified even if they are not too long, they are classified in short time and live classification is possible. Thus, we chose $b = 4$.

Packet window ($C = 80$). While we would like to keep the packet window as small as possible, the χ^2 test is considered to be statistically significant if the number of samples for each value is at least 5. Having chosen $b = 4$, in order to have $E_i = C/2^b$ equal to 5, we need C to be equal to about 80. Sensitivity to C is evaluated in the Sec.4.1.

Number of bytes per packet ($N = 12$). In general, classification accuracy increases with the number of considered bytes per packet. However, complexity of the classification tool increases also with the N, in terms of both memory and computational complexity. As a convenient trade-off we choose $N = 12$ so, given $b = 4$, this values corresponds to $G = 24$ groups for each signature. One motivation for the chosen value is because it allows to analyze the most important part of RTP and DNS headers. Even more, $N = 12$ allows to collect 20 bytes of the IP packet payload (12 bytes + 8 bytes of the UDP header) that is the minimum size of the TCP header and the typical value used by measurement tools. Notice that the optimal value of N depends from the targeted applications. For example, DNS and eMule can be clearly identified by only considering (χ_2, χ_3) as right plot of Fig. 2 shows. The selection of which groups to include in $\overline{\chi}$ is then a complex task that is left out as future work.

2.2   KISS Model Generation for Classification

The decision process in KISS is driven by a Support Vector Machine (SVM). The SVM approach is based on the idea of mapping training samples so that samples of two different classes are displaced in compact areas separated by hyperplanes. Since SVM is a supervised learning method, a training set must be used to generate the model used for the classification task. To generate a KISS model we operate as sketched in right plot of Fig. 1. We start by considering some streams that belong to a given set of applications we want to classify. The streams could either be generated on purpose (e.g., by running the applications), or extracted from real traffic traces through some other reliable classification engine. Streams are then fed into a *chunker*, whose role is to derive the KISS signatures as in (3). This signature set is than randomly sampled (according to a uniform distribution) so as to select the *training set*, whose size is 300 by default (the impact of this value will be discussed in Sec. 4.1). The training set is then fed to the SVM learning phase after which the KISS model is produced; samples used for training will not be used for the model validation.

Notice that the KISS training phase *partitions* the signature space into a number of regions equal to the number of protocol offered during the training: this implies that a sample will *always* be classified as belonging to any of the known classes. Thus, an additional region is needed to represent all samples that do not belong to any of the above protocols, i.e., to represent all the other protocols. Thus, the training set must contains two types of signatures: i) the ones referring to traffic generated by the applications to classify; ii) the ones representing all the remaining traffic, which we refer to as *Other –* which represents the set of applications that we are not interested in classifying.

3   Testing Methodology

We developed an ad-hoc oracle to derive the ground truth, that is based on DPI mechanism, and to manually tune it and to double check its performance. The oracle is used to extract desired protocols and Other protocols, which are then used as ground truth to assess KISS performance.

3.1   Testing Datasets

Real Traffic Traces (RealTrace) were collected from the network of an ISP provider in Italy called FastWeb. This network is a very heterogeneous scenario, in which users are free to use the network without any restrictions, and there is a large portion of VoIP and P2P traffic. It therefore represents a very demanding scenario considering traffic classification. A probe node has been installed in a PoP, in which more than 1000 users are connected. The measurements presented in this paper refer to a dataset collected starting from 26th of May 2006, and ending on 4th of June 2006. The trace contains 6455 millions UDP packets, 77.6 millions flows, 56368 endpoints. Among the most popular applications generating UDP traffic, we selected: i) eMule, ii) VoIP (over RTP), and iii) DNS protocols. Indeed, these three protocols alone account for more than 80% of UDP endpoints, 95% of UDP the flows, and 96% of the total UDP bitrate.

Testbed Traces (P2Ptrace) Since we are also interested in evaluating the performance of KISS when dealing with new protocols, we selected, as case study, some popular P2P-TV applications (namely PPLive, Joost, SopCast and TVants). Since none of the selected applications was available at the time of real traffic trace collection, we gather such traces with a testbed. The dataset consists of packet level traces collected from more than 40 PCs running the above mentioned P2P-TV applications in 5 different Countries, at 11 different institutions during the Napa-Wine [7] project.

DPI oracle has been implemented in Tstat [8], and its performance were manually fine tuned and double checked. In particular, for DNS we rely on simple port classification, since UDP port 53 was only used by the DNS system during 2006 whereas for RTP

Table 1. Confusion matrix considering the RealTrace case (left) and P2P-TV Applications (right)

	Tot.	RTP	eMule	DNS	Other
RTP	8389	99.9	0.05	-	0.05
eMule	7167	-	99.9	-	0.1
DNS	4491	-	-	98.7	1.3
Other	1477	-	-	-	100.0

	Tot.	Joost	PPLive	SopCast	TVants	Other
Joost	33514	98.1	-	-	-	1.9
PPLive	84452	-	100.0	-	-	-
SopCast	84473	-	-	99.9	-	0.1
TVants	27184	-	-	-	100.0	-
Other	1.2M	0.3	-	-	-	99.7

classification we rely on the state machine described in [9]. Instead for eMule the system proposed in [10,11] has been developed and adapted to the scenario[1].

4   Results

Considering RealTrace dataset, left Tab. 3.1 summarizes the results reporting the confusion matrix. Each row corresponds to a sub trace that was classified according to the oracle. Columns report the total number of samples in each class, and their corresponding percentages classified by KISS for each of the four classes. Values on the main diagonal correspond to True Positive percentage (%TP), while other values details the False Negative percentage (%FN) and False Positive percentage (%FP). For example, in the left table, the first row says that the 99.9% of samples extracted considering RTP flows only has been correctly classified by KISS (i.e., those are True Positives); the remaining 0.1% of samples has been classified as eMule and Other protocols with 0.05% each (i.e., those are False Positive considering eMule and Other classes). Overall results are astonishing. The average True Positive percentage is 99.6%, with the worst %TP equal to 98.7%, since 1.3% DNS endpoints are misclassified as Other (58 samples over 4491 tests). %FP=0.05%: all samples in the Other class has been correctly classified, while 5 RTP instances have been misclassified as eMule.

To prove the KISS flexibility, we explore its ability to identify traffic generated by P2P-TV applications. Since these are novel applications, which follow a proprietary and closed design and might exploit obfuscation and encryption techniques, the design and engineering of a DPI mechanism would be daunting and extremely expensive. On the contrary, training KISS to identify P2P-TV traffic is quite straightforward. For each considered application, a packet trace is captured by simply running the application. Those traces are then used to train the SVM. To test the KISS ability to classify P2P-TV traffic, all traces from the P2Ptrace dataset are used to evaluate the True Positive. The RealTrace is instead used to evaluate the False Positive, since we assume no P2P-TV traffic could be present during 2006. Results are summarized in the right Tab. 3.1, which reports percentages averaged over more that 1.3 millions of tests. Also in this case, results are amazing. KISS is able to correctly classify more than 98.1% of samples as True Positives in the worst case, and only 0.3% of False Positives are present.

---

[1] The eMule client used by FastWeb users has been optimized to exploit FastWeb network architecture. This entailed a modification to the KAD protocol, called KADu. Off-the-shelf DPI signatures have been then adapted to cope with the modified protocol.

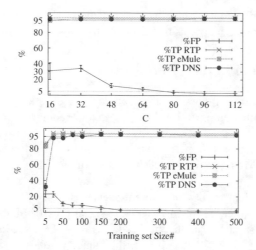

Fig. 3. Classification accuracy versus C (on the left) and versus the training set size (on the right)

4.1 Parameter Sensitivity

Among the parameters that are part of KISS, the number of samples C to evaluate the signature is the most critical one. Indeed, to have a good estimate of the observed frequencies, at least 5 samples for each value should be collected (in case a uniform distribution is considered). This leads to $C \geq 80$. However, since in KISS we are not performing a real Chi-square test, we are interested in observing the classification accuracy of KISS when reducing the number of observation and therefore allowing an earlier classification. Left plot of Fig. 3 reports the %TP of well-known protocols, and the %FP, without distinguishing among protocols. Confidence intervals are evaluated over 250 different RealTrace subtraces each comprising more than 100 samples. The Figure clearly shows that the %TP is almost not affected C. Indeed, the syntax of the considered protocols is very different and the SVM has little problem in distinguishing them even if C is small. However, the %FP is much more sensible to the C value, and only for $C > 80$ it goes below 5%. Similarly, it is interesting to observe how performance changes with training sets of different size. Results are plotted in right plot of Fig. 3, which reports the %TP and %FP for increasing training set size. The plot shows that KISS is able to correctly classify RTP, DNS and eMule traffic with excellent %TP, (average %TP>95%) even with 5 samples training sets. Also in this case, more problematic is the correct classification of the Other traffic, since the False Positive percentage goes below 5% only when the training set comprises at least 100 samples. Intuitively, the Other traffic is far more heterogeneous than traffic of a given protocol, and thus a larger number of samples are required to describe it.

Given the connectionless characteristic of UDP, one expects that connection last for few packets. Analyzing the RealTrace dataset, 40% of endpoints has only 1 packet, while only 5% have at least 80 packets. However, these latter endpoints account for more than 98% of volume in *bytes* of traffic. This clearly shows that, while KISS is not suitable for the classification of short-lived connections, it can however successfully target the small fraction of endpoints that generate the large majority of traffic.

5   Conclusions and Future Works

We presented KISS, a novel classifier that couples a stochastic description of applications to the discrimination power of Support Vector Machines. Signatures are automatically extracted from a traffic stream by the means of stochastic test that allows application protocol syntax to emerge, while ignoring protocol synchronization and semantic rules. A SVM is then used to classify the extracted signatures, leading to exceptional performance.

KISS showed excellent results in different scenarios, considering both data, VoIP, and P2P filesharing applications. Moreover, KISS also provide almost perfect results when facing new P2P streaming applications, such as Joost, PPLive, SopCast and TVants. Compared to classic DPI, KISS is more flexible, since it relies on a statistical characterization of application layer protocol payload, therefore being robust to protocol evolution/dialects, eventual packet reordering/losses or sampling.

On the other side, the classification results are strongly related to the ground truth used to train the SVM classifier. This is particularly true for the background class which should represent all protocols that are not the target of classification. This set of protocols can change in time so that a static trainset can become "outdated". The same problem exists even for well known applications because is difficult to cover all the possible behaviour of an application. This suggest the need of a loopback in the model creation so that the trainset can be adapted accordingly the traffic changes. These is something we are interested of studying in the future.

Another possible optimization is the application of a feature selection algorithm to identify the most significant chi-square features. This should speed up the computation time of the signatures and decrease the memory requirements.

The classification method proposed is applied only on UDP traffic but, even with some restrictions, it can also be applied to TCP. In this case, due to the connection oriented nature of TCP, the signature can be computed using only the first(s) segment(s) of each flow. This subject is already under investigation but is outside the scope of this paper.

References

1. Karagiannis, T., Broido, A., Brownlee, N., Claffy, K.C., Faloutsos, M.: Is P2P dying or just hiding? In: IEEE GLOBECOM 2004, November 2004, vol. 3, pp. 1532–1538 (2004)
2. Bonfiglio, D., Mellia, M., Meo, M., Rossi, D., Tofanelli, P.: Revealing Skype Traffic: when Randomness Plays with You. In: ACM SIGCOMM, Kyoto, JP (August 2007)
3. Karagiannis, T., Papagiannaki, K., Faloutsos, M.: BLINC: multilevel traffic classification in the dark. ACM SIGCOMM Computer Communication Review 35(4) (2005)
4. Moore, A.W., Zuev, D.: Internet traffic classification using bayesian analysis techniques. In: ACM SIGMETRICS, Banff, Canada, June 2005, pp. 50–60 (2005)
5. Cristianini, N., Shawe-Taylor, J.: An introduction to support Vector Machines and other kernel-based learning methods. Cambridge University Press, New York (1999)

6. Wang, R., Liu, Y., Yang, Y., Zhou, X.: Solving the App-Level Classification Problem of P2P Traffic Via Optimized Support Vector Machines. In: Proc. of ISDA 2006 (October 2006)
7. Leonardi, E., Mellia, M., Horvart, A., Muscariello, L., Niccolini, S., Rossi, D.: Building a Cooperative P2P-TV Application over a Wise Network: the Approach of the European FP-7 STREP NAPA-WINE. IEEE Communications Magazine 46, 20–211 (2008)
8. Mellia, M., Lo Cigno, R., Neri, F.: Measuring IP and TCP behavior on edge nodes with Tstat. Computer Networks 47(1), 1–21 (2005)
9. Birke, R., Mellia, M., Petracca, M., Rossi, D.: Understanding VoIP from Backbone Measurements. In: IEEE INFOCOM 2007, Anchorage, Ak (May 2007)
10. IPP2P home page, http://www.ipp2p.org/
11. Kulbak, Y., Bickson, D.: The eMule protocol specification, Technical Report Leibniz Center TR-2005-03, School of Computer Science and Engineering, The Hebrew University (2005)

DTS: A Decentralized Tracing System

Kenji Masui[1] and Benoit Donnet[2],[*]

[1] Tokyo Institute of Technology
kmasui@gsic.titech.ac.jp
[2] Université catholique de Louvain
benoit.donnet@uclouvain.be

Abstract. A new generation of widely distributed systems to measure the Internet topology at the interface level is currently being deployed. Co-operation between monitors in these systems is required in order to avoid over-consumption of network resources. This paper proposes an architecture for a distributed topology measurement (DTM) system that, for the first time, decentralizes probing information. The key idea of our proposal is that, by utilizing a shared database as a communication method among monitors and taking advantage of the characteristics of the Doubletree algorithm, we can get rid of a specific control point, and a DTM system can be constructed in a decentralized manner. In this paper, we describe our implementation of a DTM, called Decentralized Tracing System (DTS). Decentralization within DTS is achieved using various distributed hash tables (DHTs), each one being dedicated to a particular plane (i.e., control or data). We also provide preliminary evaluation results.

1 Introduction

The past ten years have seen a growing body of important research work on the Internet topology [1]. The work is based on maps built by systems such as *Archipelago* [2], probing the Internet topology from multiple vantage points using the technique of *traceroute*. We call these *distributed topology measurement* (*DTM*) systems. Large-scale DTM systems are attracting researchers' attention due to their better capabilities of tracking network dynamics. Given we have more number of monitors for probing specific networks, each monitor can take a smaller portion of the topology and probe it more frequently. Changes that might be missed by smaller systems can more readily be captured by the larger ones, while keeping the workload per monitor constant. However, building such a large structure leads to potential scaling issues: the quantity of probes launched might consume undue network resources and the probes sent from many vantage points might appear as a distributed denial-of-service (DDoS) attack on end-hosts [3,4]. The NSF-sponsored CONMI Workshop [5] urged a comprehensive approach to distributed probing, with a shared infrastructure that respects the many security concerns that active measurements raise. DTMs must coordinate the efforts of their individual monitors.

---

[*] Benoit Donnet is funded by the Fonds National de la Recherche Scientifique (FNRS – Rue d'Egmont 5, 1000 Brussels).

M. Papadopouli, P. Owezarski, and A. Pras (Eds.): TMA 2009, LNCS 5537, pp. 126–134, 2009.
© Springer-Verlag Berlin Heidelberg 2009

In this paper, we propose the first decentralized architecture for a DTM, called *Decentralized Tracing System* (DTS). We build on our prior work [3] in introducing cooperation among tracing monitors, through the *Doubletree* topology discovery algorithm. Doubletree takes advantage of the tree-like structure of routes, either emanating from a single source to multiple destinations or routes converging from multiple sources to a single destination, in order to avoid duplication of effort for topology discovery. With Doubletree, tracing monitors cooperate by exchanging information about which interfaces were previously discovered through probing specific interfaces. Doubletree describes what must be shared but, prior to this work, we did not specify precisely how it should be shared in a distributed environment.

Our DTS makes use of a storage built on the technique of distributed hash table (DHT) for decentralizing its *control* and *data* planes. Moreover, because of the uncertain environment that DTMs must run in, where host machines are susceptible to varying network load and possible disconnection, they require an architecture that is not just scalable, but is also flexible and robust. We also consider these matters on designing DTS (Sec. 2), and discuss the preliminary evaluation of DTS (Sec. 3). Our implementation is freely available.[1]

2   Design and Implementation of DTS

2.1   DTM Systems Requirements

Control Plane. The *control plane* of a DTM system refers to the management of information regarding probing targets as well as information needed to decide when probing must stop for a given target.

First, a DTM system has to share the target list, i.e., the list of IP addresses (or names) of probe targets, between probing monitors. A target list must be permanent in the system. However, one must have the opportunity to perform on the fly some changes in the list, such as adding or removing items. For instance, a target can refuse to be probed in the future and its IP address must be then blacklisted and removed from the current target list. For the rest of this paper, we refer to the target list as *probing target* (*PT*).

Second, a DTM system has to share information to guide probing in order to make measurements more efficient. This information can help a probing monitor to decide when to stop probing a given target. By definition, such an information is volatile. In the following, we refer to this information as *probing control information* (*PC*).

A DTM system must be *dynamic*. It should accept dynamic arrivals and departures (volunteer or not) of monitors. Monitors join and leave the system when they wish (*flexibility*). Such a dynamic behavior must have limited impact on the shared information (*robustness*).

Finally, the control plane of a DTM system must ensure that each probing monitor can perform measurements at its own pace. A slower monitor cannot slowdown others monitors, which is another property for *flexibility*.

---

[1] See http://www.n-tap.net/

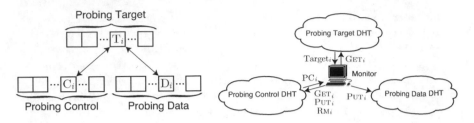

Fig. 1.   Relationship   between   **Fig. 2.** DTS and the dedicated DHTs
shared information

Data Plane. The *data plane* of a DTM system refers to the topological data collected during probing. In the fashion of the Archipelago data, the result data set should be accessible by the research community. A DTM system has to keep track of each probing result, for each probing monitor, from the beginning and must ensure the long-term persistence of this data set.

The DTM system must provide an easy access to the data storage system. On the one hand, probing monitors must be able to efficiently and easily store the data collected so that the whole system avoids a bottleneck issue when storing data. On the other hand, the information must be easily retrieved for research purposes. In the following, we refer to the collected data as *probing data* (*PD*).

2.2   Design and Implementation

In this section, we describe the *Decentralized Tracing System* (DTS), the first entirely distributed topology discovery system, and explain how our implementation meets the requirements provided in Sec. 2.1.

Previous works on Internet topology discovery include, among others, *DIMES* [6] (publicly released as a daemon), *Rocketfuel* [7] (focusing on the topology of a given ISP), *Scriptroute* [8] (a system that allows an ordinary Internet user to perform network measurements from several distributed vantage points), and *iPlane* [9] (construction of an annotated map of the Internet). All of these systems operate under central control. Indeed, unlike DTS, Rocketfuel and Scriptroute assume a centralized server to share stopping information (i.,e., the list of previously observed IP addresses). Rocketfuel and Scriptroute do not consider how the information regarding where to stop probing can be efficiently encoded for exchange between monitors.

Global View of DTS. In Sec. 2.1, we explained that a DTM system has to share information for controlling probing but also for managing the data. DTS, our implementation of a DTM system, requires three information to be shared among monitors: the probing control information, the probing target, and the probing data.

Sharing probing target and probing control information between a large set of monitors might lead to scaling issues. For instance, it could be a problem if all the monitors try to access the probing control information (or a particular item of the probing control information) at the same time. Further, if all the monitors probe the entire destination list at the same time, it is difficult to benefit from work performed by others and, consequently, difficult to exchange probing control information. A way to avoid such a problem would be to divide the target list into *chunks*. A chunk is a portion of the entire target list and there is no overlapping between chunks. Each monitor focuses, at a given time, on its own chunk. To each probing target chunk is associated a specific probing information chunk and a specific probing data chunk. Fig. 1 illustrates the relationship between a specific probing target chunk, T_i, the related information used to guide probing, C_i, and the topological data collected by monitors, D_i.

The key idea of DTS is to enable communication between monitors through the use of DHTs. For any information to share, DTS employs a dedicated DHT. Given that each DTS monitor has to share three information, the whole system requires three different DHTs, as depicted in Fig. 2.

Each value stored by a specific DHT refers to a chunk. For instance, the Probing Target DHT on Fig. 2 stores target chunks. Further, a key in a DHT will serve as the identifier for a particular chunk. For consistency reasons, the key for a target chunk is the same that the key for the corresponding probing information and data. To this end, a number is associated to each chunk and the key of the chunk is calculated based on this number.

Control Plane. The control plane of DTS is composed of several modules that interact through the *Agent* engine.

A DTS monitor probes the network with its *Prober* engine, which implements the Doubletree algorithm that is based on both backwards and forwards probing as well as the stop sets [3]. The control plane of DTS interacts with the PC DHT in order to store and retrieve the stop set corresponding to the current chunk.

Our approach in constructing DTS is somewhat similar to Chawathe et al. [10] who evaluate whether it is possible to use DHTs as an application-independent building block to implement a key component of an end-user positioning system. DTS is a DTM system that makes use of DHTs to share information between monitors. One of the key ideas we had in mind when designing DTS was its ease of deployment. We therefore choose to make DTS free from DHT specifications. Instead, we provide a *DHT Abstraction* engine, making the DHT transparent to a monitor as it interacts only with the DHT Abstraction. In particular, the DHT Abstraction engine interacts with the interfaces provided by N-TAP [11]. These interfaces allow other systems to utilize the features of N-TAP including the shared database and communication channels among monitors. The DHT Abstraction engine converts the information that are exchanged between the control plane and N-TAP so that it can provide consistent interfaces to other modules in DTS.

Data Plane. Our implementation of the data plane is somewhat similar to the control plane. The difference stands in the fact that the Prober engine is replaced by a *Data* engine. The objective of the Data engine is to transform the raw replies (i.e., ICMP received) into well formatted data that contains

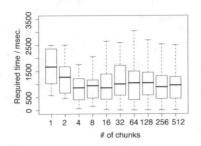

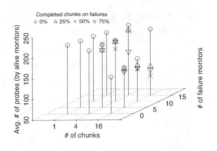

Fig. 3. Required time for retrieving one chunk from PT DHT

Fig. 4. Impact of the failure of monitors and the chunk size on the number of probes

additional information useful for the research community, such as timestamps, stopping reasons, DTS monitor name, chunk identifier, etc.. The collected data is, then, sent through the DHT abstraction to the PD DHT.

Adaptation to N-TAP. According to the design presented so far, we describe how DTS is implemented on an existing measurement platform, N-TAP [11]. Basically, the N-TAP platform consists of *N-TAP agents* that are assumed to reside in multiple administrative domains. Besides the agents perform measurement, the agents also play a role in forming a measurement overlay network with the technique of Chord [12]. The overlay network is called the *N-TAP network*, which provides some high-level functions such as shared database among agents. In N-TAP, there are two roles of agents: *core* and *stub* [13]. The core agents have to maintain a Chord-based peer-to-peer network for its DHT service, meanwhile, the stub agents do not need to maintain the network but join the network via a core agent. These two kinds of agents form a bi-layered peer-to-peer network.

For constructing the DTS, we prepare several stable nodes as core agents that can serve the shared database. Since the number of the core agents has an impact on the scalability of DTS, we should carefully choose the number. On the other hand, in principle, DTS monitors play a role of a stub agent and do not engage in the maintenance of the DHT service. The monitors, of course, perform topology discovery based on the Doubletree algorithm, and can utilize the dedicated DHTs (for PC/PT/PD) via a core agent. Briefly, core agents work as a gateway of the DHT service for stub agents.

3   Evaluation

The decentralized architecture of DTS, which is based on the DHT-based storage and the intercommunication among monitors via the storage (not the direct communication among the monitors), provides some advantages. We can summarize them with four points: flexibility, robustness, scalability, and modularity. The robustness in DTS is related to the impact of monitor failures. When a monitor (or several monitors) fails, the entire system must continue to work. Further, the information lost (probing data and probing control) due to the failure must be limited. In this section, we evaluate the robustness of DTS through the impact of the chunk size and monitor failure.

Even though DTS can maintain its function, the failure of monitors causes the loss of data that are expected to be collected by the failed monitors. With the scheme of chunks, the impact of data loss depends on the chunk size: larger the chunks, larger the loss. Since collected data are handled in a unit of a chunk and committed to the shared database after a monitor finishes working on the chunk, the failure of a monitor causes the loss of the collected data contained in a working chunk. Such a data loss can be avoided by making chunks smaller, however, this will increase the burdens on monitors due to more frequent interaction with the shared database. Therefore, the chunk size is an important factor to decide the robustness of DTS.

In order to investigate the relationship between the chunk size and the interaction with the shared database, we first performed an experiment that invokes the handle of various sizes of chunks. We randomly chose 16 PlanetLab nodes and deployed DTS on them. These nodes are set to the core agents that form a DHT-based database. We also prepared a probing target list that contains 1024 valid IPv4 addresses, and evenly divided them into C chunks $(C = 2^i; i = 1, 2, ..., 9)$, i.e., each chunk contains $1024/C$ IP addresses. These chunks were stored in the PT DHT. In respective cases, we made all monitors retrieve all chunks from the PT DHT and recorded the monitors behavior.

Fig. 3 illustrates the distribution of required time among all monitors for retrieving one chunk in the respective cases of C. In this figure, the bottom and top of a box respectively show the 25th and 75th percentiles of the required time, and a bold line across a box shows the median value. The ends of a whisker indicate the minimum and maximum values except for the outliers that lie more than 1.5 times IQR (inter-quartile range) lower than the 25th percentile or 1.5 times IQR higher than the 75th percentile. One can see that the required time decreases as the chunk number increases from 1 to 4, however the time just shows a slight change from $C = 4$ to $C = 512$. This is because a dominant element in the required time switches between the chunk size and the overhead caused by the interaction with the PT DHT. In DTS, chunks are exchanged based on the N-TAP's messaging protocol. An N-TAP message usually contains a 16-byte length header, a 47-byte length additional header, and user data. The message is transmitted by TCP. The length of user data increases by 10 bytes per one target IPv4 address. Therefore, the length of the received message for retrieving one chunk is $(63 + 10240/C)$ bytes. Up to $C = 4$, when the message length was 2,623 bytes or more, the dominant part of the required time was the time for transferring a considerable length of a message that contains a chunk. When the value of C was larger than 4, the message length became short enough, meanwhile, the overhead that derives from a routing procedure in DHT cannot be ignored compared to the time for transferring a message.

Then how the chunk size affects the overall workload in the case of the failure of monitors? This is also a considerable problem because DTS ensures monitors' arbitrary joining and leaving and must also be robust to unexpected events, such as monitor failure. In order to deal with this problem, we conducted an experiment that involve the failure of some monitors in process of probing.

For the experiment, we randomly selected 16 PlanetLab nodes that reside in different sites, and deployed DTS on these nodes. We also selected other 16 PlanetLab nodes as probing targets. Then we made the monitors perform the procedures for topology discovery to these targets. We prepared three sizes for chunks: one chunk, 4 chunks, and 16 chunks for 16 targets (these chunks contain the same number of targets without overlapping). Some of the monitors were configured to fail and unexpectedly leave the system at one of these timings: when a monitor performed no probe (0 %), or when a monitor completed probes for 25 %, 50 %, or 75 % of chunks. For example, the proportion of 25 % in the case of 4 chunks means that a monitor fails after it finishes topology probing for one of 4 chunks. We also changed the number of failed monitors between 0, 5, 10, and 15, where the value of 0 means that all monitors finished probing without failure. After the rest of the monitors, i.e., alive monitors, have finished topology discovery to the targets, we looked into the number of probes performed by the alive monitors.

Fig. 4 indicates the number of probes performed on each condition. The number of probes shown in this figure is the average values of the probes performed by alive monitors. From these values, we can find how the failure of monitors on each condition affects the overall workload in DTS. We note that, in the case that the number of chunks is 1, the plots when the proportion of completed chunks is 25 %, 50 %, or 75 % are not shown, because the monitors have only one chunk to handle.

One significant point is that, when monitors have just one chunk, the number of probes scarcely changes depending the number of failed monitors. In this case, the failure of a monitor causes the complete loss of the data collected by the monitor because the data are not committed to the shared database until the monitor finishes the work for only one chunk.

We can also see that, in the case of the number of failure monitors is 15 and the proportion of completed chunks is 0 %, the number of probes shows little change against the variation of the number of chunks. This is because only one monitor kept alive and other monitors failed without probing, the alive monitor cannot take advantage of the global stop sets originated by other monitors. As a result, the merit of the Doubletree algorithm decreases, and the efficiency of topology discovery by the alive monitor was not improved so much. Except for the cases that the number of failure monitors is 15, the number of probes decreases as the chunk size becomes smaller (i. e., the larger number of chunks). This means that the smaller chunk size ensures more rapid reflection to the global stop sets, which results in the utilization of the stop sets from other monitors.

Additionally, even if monitors fail, the chunks that the failed monitors have already completed contribute to the overall efficiency of topology discovery. As seen in this figure, the higher proportion of completed chunks basically decreases the number of probes more. Especially in the cases where the proportion of completed chunks is 50 % or more, its impact is notable. The reason why we see it brings a bigger impact on the number of probes when the number of chunks is larger (16) will be similar to the one stated in the previous paragraph.

As stated above, the smaller chunk size has the effect of decreasing the overall number of probes. Meanwhile, it increases the number of DHT storage accesses, which will keep monitors waiting until its procedures finish. For more rapid and accurate grasping of the Internet topology, we are now working at the analysis of this trade-off.

4   Conclusion

Current systems for discovering the Internet topology at the IP interface level are undergoing a radical shift. Whereas the present generation of systems operates on largely dedicated hosts, numbering between 20 and 200, a new generation of easily downloadable measurement software means that infrastructures based on thousands of hosts could spring up literally overnight. These systems must be carefully engineered in order to avoid abuse and duplication of efforts between tracing monitors. To this end, monitors must share information to guide probing. We stated, in this paper, that this sharing must be decentralized in order to be, among others, scalable and robust. We identified the needs of such a system and discuss how we implement them into what is, to the best of our knowledge, the first fully decentralized tracing system. We are currently exploring the possibilities of our implementation through the investigation of basic characteristics of DTS deployed on the PlanetLab testbed.

References

1. Donnet, B., Friedman, T.: Internet topology discovery: a survey. IEEE Communications Surveys and Tutorials 9(4), 2–15 (2007)
2. Claffy, K., Hyun, Y., Keys, K., Fomenkov, M.: Internet mapping: from art to science. In: Proc. IEEE CATCH (March 2009)
3. Donnet, B., Raoult, P., Friedman, T., Crovella, M.: Efficient algorithms for large-scale topology discovery. In: Proc. ACM SIGMETRICS (June 2005)
4. Spring, N., Wetherall, D., Anderson, T.: Reverse-engineering the internet. In: Proc. HotNets-II (November 2003)
5. Claffy, K., Crovella, M., Friedman, T., Shannon, C., Spring, N.: Community-oriented network measurement infrastructure (COMNI) workshop report. ACM SIGCOMM Computer Communication Review 36(2), 41–48 (2006)
6. Shavitt, Y., Shir, E.: DIMES: Let the internet measure itself. ACM SIGCOMM Computer Communication Review 35(5) (October 2005)
7. Spring, N., Mahajan, R., Wetherall, D.: Measuring ISP topologies with Rocketfuel. In: Proc. ACM SIGCOMM (August 2002)
8. Spring, N., Wetherall, D., Anderson, T.: Scriptroute: A public internet measurement facility. In: Proc. USENIX USITS (March 2002)
9. Madhyastha, H.V., Isdal, T., Piatek, M., Dixon, C., Anderson, T., Krishnamurthy, A., Venkataramani, A.: iPlane: An information plance for distributed services. In: Proc. USENIX OSDI (November 2006)

10. Chawathe, Y., Ramabhadran, S., Ratnasamy, S., LaMarca, A., Shenker, S., Heller-stein, J.: A case study in building layered DHT applications. In: Proc. ACM SIG-COMM (August 2005)
11. Masui, K., Kadobayashi, Y.: N-TAP: A platform of large-scale distributed mea-surement for overlay network applications. In: Proc. DAS-P2P (January 2007)
12. Stoica, I., Morris, R., Liben-Nowell, D., Karger, D., Kaashoek, M.F., Dabek, F., Balakrishnan, H.: Chord: A scalable peer-to-peer lookup service for internet appli-cations. IEEE Transactions on Networking (ToN) 11(1), 17–32 (2003)
13. Masui, K., Kadobayashi, Y.: A role-based peer-to-peer approach to application-oriented measurement platforms. In: Fdida, S., Sugiura, K. (eds.) AINTEC 2007. LNCS, vol. 4866, pp. 184–198. Springer, Heidelberg (2007)

Author Index